MW01611186

The Finished Work of Christ:
Establishing His Kingdom Within

Bobby Joe Jones

BookLocker

Trenton, Georgia

Copyright © 2025 Bobby Joe Jones

Paperback ISBN: 978-1-961265-07-3
Hardcover ISBN: 978-1-961265-08-0
Ebook ISBN: 979-8-88532-165-5

All rights reserved. No part of this publication may be reproduced, stored in a retrieval system, or transmitted in any form or by any means, electronic, mechanical, recording or otherwise, without the prior written permission of the author.

Published by BookLocker.com, Inc., Trenton, Georgia.

BookLocker.com, Inc.
2025

First Edition

Library of Congress Cataloging in Publication Data
Jones, Bobby Joe
The Finished Work of Christ: Establishing His Kingdom Within
by Bobby Joe Jones
Library of Congress Control Number: 2025921589

www.FinishedWorkofChrist.com

Table of Contents

This book is dedicated to

"My Father"

The Finished Work of Christ: Establishing His Kingdom Within

 **Forward**

This began as a fire in my chest.
Not because I was angry—but because I was undone.
Not because I wanted to fix the church—but because I longed to honor Jesus.

The gospel I inherited was transactional, delayed, institutional, and guilt-soaked.
But the Jesus I met was honest, present, relational, and radical.
His love didn't just change me—it ruined me for anything less.

What follows is not just another teaching or sermon series.
It is a confrontation of distortion, and a revelation of reality.
It is not written to please theologians—but to honor the King.
It's not a new gospel—it's a fresh witness to the finished one.

I call it a manifesto—but really, it's a mirror.
It reflects what many already believe but have lacked words to say.
It names what has been buried under doctrine and dogma, and it calls a generation into reality. It deconstructs religious striving

and replaces it with Spirit-led rest. It commissions readers into a new world, fully aligned with the reign of Christ already within them.

The kingdom has come.
The reign has begun.
The work is finished.

Now we live it.

The Finished Work of Christ: Establishing His Kingdom Within

Preface: The Love That Fueled It All

Before there was action—there was affection. Every moment of Christ's mission was a response to the eternal love of the Father. Creation itself was born from it. Redemption was planned through it. Restoration flows from it.

John 3:16— "For God so loved the world that He gave His only Son..."
Romans 5:8— "But God demonstrates His own love toward us..."
Ephesians 2:4–5— "Because of His great love... He made us alive with Christ."
2 Corinthians 5:14— "For the love of Christ compels us..."

What love does:

- Gives freely without condition

- Pursues relentlessly without threat

- Empowers change without coercion

- Restores dignity without hierarchy

- Never fails, never ends, never loses

Insight: Love is not the background—it's the blueprint. The finished work is what love looks like when it's not withheld.

Introduction: Not Just a Story—A Revolution of Reality

This is not mythology. It's not poetry or distant parable. It's a reality-altering announcement: the life, death, resurrection, ascension, enthronement of Jesus—and the giving of the Holy Spirit—are not chapters waiting for interpretation. They are the completed unveiling of God's plan for humanity.

No temple veil remains. No distance endures. What was finished then is alive now. He did not come to start a religion. He did not come to appease the Father. He did not rise to reclaim a throne He never lost. He came to establish His kingdom—within us.

John 17:4 — "I have glorified You on the earth. I have finished the work which You have given Me to do."
John 19:30 — "It is finished."
Hebrews 10:10 — "We have been sanctified through the offering of the body of Jesus Christ once for all."

That kingdom is not waiting. It's not postponed. It's not reserved for the end of time or hidden in mystery. It is here. Now. Inside. Through the finished work of Jesus Christ

---

1. His Life — The Revelation of the Father

Jesus did not come to change God's mind about us. He came to reveal that God's mind had never changed. Jesus didn't come to rescue us from the Father. He came to introduce us to Him. He was the exact representation of God's being. He lived with radical clarity and relentless compassion—not as an exception to humanity, but as the true model of it.

He embodied the full expression of divine love and human dignity. No title, rule, or institution could contain the radical freedom He embodied. His compassion rewrote social norms, His forgiveness shattered cycles of shame, and His inclusion dismantled hierarchy.

John 14:9 — "If you've seen Me, you've seen the Father."
John 10:10 — "I came that they may have life, and have it abundantly."
Isaiah 53:3–5 — The suffering servant bore our griefs and carried our sorrows.
Luke 4:18–19 — He came to proclaim liberty, healing, and restoration.

What He did:

- He healed without conditions.

- He restored worth to the rejected.

- He called ordinary people into extraordinary purpose.

- He challenged religious gatekeeping and political power structures.

- He elevated the poor, the outcast, and the sinner to places of honor.

Insight: His sinless life fulfilled the Law perfectly (*Hebrews 4:15*), qualifying Him as the spotless Lamb. Jesus lived as the perfect revelation of the Father—a human fully alive in love, justice, and dignity. His life wasn't just exemplary; it was the blueprint for what we were always meant to be: beloved children hosting divine presence.

---

2. His Death: Love's Ultimate Triumph

The cross was not a tragedy—it was the moment when love conquered distortion, shame, and separation. The cross was not God's wrath poured out—it was love poured out. He did not die to rescue us from His Father—but to unite us with Him. He did not die to make salvation possible—He died to complete it. Jesus absorbed the distortion of humanity and buried it in His death. It was not payment—it was restoration.

2 Corinthians 5:19— "God was in Christ reconciling the world to Himself..."
Colossians 2:14— "He canceled the record of debt... nailing it to the cross."
Romans 6:6— "Our old self was crucified with Him..."

John 12:32 — "When I am lifted up... I will draw all people to Myself.

John 19:30 — "It is finished."

Hebrews 9:12 — "He entered once for all... by means of His own blood."

Colossians 1:20 — "Making peace by the blood of His cross."

1 Peter 3:18 — "Christ suffered once for sins... to bring us to God."

Romans 6:10 — "He died to sin once for all."

What He accomplished:

- Fulfilled the Old Covenant sacrificial system

- Removed all barriers between God and humanity

- Reconciled all things through mercy, not wrath

- Declared the end of condemnation and the beginning of divine embrace

Insight: His death was a once-for-all act, ending all need for further sacrifice (*Hebrews 10:12*). Judgment was poured out—what remains is mercy.

The cross wasn't an instrument of divine wrath—it was the triumph of self-emptying love. Jesus absorbed the worst of human distortion and, through love, rendered it powerless. Death didn't win. Hierarchy didn't win. Empire didn't win. Love won.

The cry "It is finished" echoes not as a conclusion, but as the commissioning of a love-fueled, kingdom-driven humanity.

---

3. His Resurrection: Reality Rewritten

The empty tomb is not symbolic—it is seismic. The resurrection was not a reversal—it was a re-creation. Death was not just defeated; it was dethroned. The enemy didn't just lose the fight—the enemy was disarmed, exposed, and stripped of all authority.

Romans 6:9 — "Christ, being raised from the dead, will never die again; death no longer has dominion over Him."
1 Corinthians 15:22 — "As in Adam all die, so in Christ all will be made alive."
Romans 4:25 — "He was delivered for our offenses and raised for our justification."
Acts 13:38–39 — "Through Him everyone who believes is freed from all things."
Colossians 2:15 — "Having disarmed the powers and authorities, He made a public spectacle of them, triumphing over them by the cross."
Hebrews 2:14 — "...that through death He might destroy the one who has the power of death—that is, the devil."

What He did:

- Appeared to hundreds (*1 Corinthians 15:6*)

- Ate, walked, and spoke to His followers

- Commissioned them with authority, not fear

- Broke the claim of darkness over humanity

- Crushed the power of accusation, shame, and fear

- Unveiled a kingdom that no longer negotiates with death

Insight: The resurrection validates the entire redemptive plan (*1 Corinthians 15:17*). It redefines what it means to be human: not bound by sin or shame, not intimidated by spiritual powers—but reborn in divine image, equipped to walk in fullness and freedom. Rising from the grave wasn't just personal vindication—it was the eruption of new creation. The Resurrection of Jesus confirms that distortion doesn't have the final word, and that we are invited into life beyond the confines of sin and power structures.

---

4. His Ascension: Heaven Touches Earth

Jesus didn't disappear—He ascended to reign. His departure was not abandonment but enthronement. He exchanged proximity for permanence—within us.

Matthew 28:18— "All authority... has been given to Me."
Acts 1:9— "He was taken up before their eyes."
Ephesians 4:10— "He ascended... to fill all things."

Hebrews 1:3— "He sat down at the right hand of the Majesty on high."

Insight: His ascension marks the completion of His earthly mission and the beginning of His heavenly intercession (*Hebrews 7:25*). Jesus didn't leave us—He relocated authority. The ascension is His enthronement, not His absence. It signals the beginning of a new age where heaven's reign flows through human vessels, not religious institutions.

---

5. His Enthronement: The Reign Has Begun

Jesus is not waiting to reign—He reigns now. The throne is not reserved—it is occupied.

Hebrews 10:12— "He sat down at the right hand of God."
Psalm 110:1— "Sit at My right hand..."
Ephesians 1:20–22— Christ is seated above all rule and authority.

Insight: His seated position means the work is done—there's nothing left to earn. The increase of His government and peace will never stop (*Isaiah 9:7*). It is unstoppable, world-changing, driven by love. Christ is not waiting to be crowned. He is reigning now, from the inside out—through Spirit-filled sons and daughters who manifest divine will on earth. His kingdom expands through love, justice, and restoration, not domination and coercion.

---

6. The Sending of the Spirit: The Indwelling of Jesus

Pentecost was not the birth of a religion—it was the unleashing of divine life. Jesus didn't just send power; He sent Himself in Spirit-form to dwell within humanity. The Spirit is not a force or a feeling—it is the indwelling presence of Jesus, the fulfillment of His promise: *"I will not leave you as orphans; I will come to you"* (*John 14:18*).

John 14:16–17 — "I will ask the Father, and He will give you another Helper... He dwells with you and will be in you."
Acts 2:1–4 — The Spirit came with wind and fire, filling every believer.
Acts 2:16–17 — Peter declares, "This is what was spoken by the prophet Joel..."
Romans 8:9–11 — "If Christ is in you... the Spirit gives life."
1 Corinthians 6:19 — "Your body is a temple of the Holy Spirit."
Galatians 4:6 — "God sent the Spirit of His Son into our hearts, crying, 'Abba, Father!'"

What happened at Pentecost:

- Jesus ascended, and the Spirit descended—not as a substitute, but as continuation

- The Spirit came not just upon people, but into them

- The apostles recognized and proclaimed that this was the fulfillment of Jesus' promise

- The Spirit democratized divine access—no longer limited to prophets or priests

- The law moved from stone tablets to human hearts (*Jeremiah 31:33*)

- The Spirit became the new covenant seal, the internal witness of sonship

Insight: Pentecost marks the transition from transaction to transformation. The old system was exterior, conditional, and hierarchical. The new reality is interior, relational, and universal. The Spirit doesn't negotiate—it recreates. The Spirit doesn't visit—it inhabits. This was the moment the age of the Spirit began. The Spirit is not a postscript to the gospel—it is the proof of it. Pentecost wasn't a spiritual fireworks show—it was the continuation of incarnation. Christ now lives within us. We are the body, the dwelling place, the emissaries of the kingdom. The Spirit empowers radical love and divine clarity. Jesus didn't just die and rise to forgive sin; He did so to make room for Himself within us. Pentecost is the moment that room was filled.

---

7. Who We Became: Spirit-Born Identity

Pentecost didn't just change the atmosphere—it changed us.

The Spirit didn't come to improve our behavior; He came to redefine our being. We are no longer outsiders trying to earn favor—we are sons and daughters, indwelt by the very presence of Christ.

Galatians 4:6–7 — "Because you are sons, God sent the Spirit of His Son into our hearts... So you are no longer a slave, but a son."
Romans 8:15–16 — "You have received the Spirit of adoption... The Spirit Himself testifies with our spirit that we are children of God."
2 Corinthians 5:17 — "If anyone is in Christ, he is a new creation."
Ephesians 1:13–14 — "You were marked in Him with a seal, the promised Holy Spirit... a deposit guaranteeing our inheritance."
1 Peter 2:9 — "You are a chosen people, a royal priesthood, a holy nation, God's special possession."

Who we became:

- Temples of divine presence — no longer visiting God, but hosting Him

- Adopted heirs — not just forgiven, but family

- New creations — not improved versions, but entirely reborn

- Ambassadors of heaven — carrying the kingdom within us

- Unified body — diverse members, one Spirit, one mission

- Living witnesses — our lives now echo the resurrection

Insight: The Spirit doesn't just dwell in us—He testifies through us. Our identity is no longer shaped by history, failure, or fear. It is shaped by indwelling glory. Pentecost was the moment heaven moved in—and we became the evidence. We are not sinners trying to be saints. We are co-heirs of a present kingdom, carriers of glory, citizens of heaven here and now. Our identity is not defined by lack but by abundance—from the Father's perspective, not religion's rules.

---

8. What This Means: Spirit-Shaped Mission and Community

The indwelling Spirit doesn't just transform individuals—it reconfigures reality.

Pentecost was the beginning of a new humanity, a Spirit-filled people who embody the love, justice, and healing of Jesus in the world. The church is no longer a building or institution—it is a living organism, animated by divine breath.

Acts 2:42–47 — The Spirit-filled community shared everything, broke bread, and lived in awe
Romans 12:4–5 — "We are one body in Christ, and individually members of one another."
1 Corinthians 12:7 — "To each is given the manifestation of the Spirit for the common good."
James 5:16 — "Pray for one another... The prayer of a righteous person is powerful and effective."

Micah 6:8 — "Do justice, love mercy, walk humbly with your God."

What this means for us:

- Mission is now incarnational — we carry Christ into every space we enter

- Healing flows through us — physical, emotional, relational restoration is part of our witness

- Justice is non-negotiable — the Spirit convicts and empowers us to confront oppression

- Community becomes sacred — every believer is a priest, every gathering a sanctuary

- Ecclesiology is redefined — the church is not a hierarchy, but a Spirit-led fellowship

- Love becomes the law — not rules, but relationship; not control, but compassion

Insight: Pentecost didn't just empower the apostles—it commissioned a people. The Spirit-filled church is the visible expression of the invisible kingdom. We are not waiting for heaven—we are revealing it. The church is not a place or a hierarchy—it is a Spirit-born family living out divine love. Our mission is restoration, dignity, and creative healing. Every person, every culture, every neighborhood becomes a context for kingdom expression.

9. From Inside Us—Outward

Everything Jesus finished was meant to be experienced, not awaited. The kingdom is not institutional—it's incarnational.

Luke 17:21— "The kingdom of God is within you."
Colossians 1:27— "Christ in you, the hope of glory."
1 Corinthians 6:19— "Your body is a temple of the Holy Spirit."
2 Corinthians 5:18 — "God... gave us the ministry of reconciliation."

You become:

- A living temple

- A carrier of glory

- An agent of reconciliation

- A walking image of love over control, peace over fear, dignity over hierarchy

Insight: The finished work joins us to Christ's death and resurrection, enabling us to walk in the reality of new life (*Romans 6:4*). The transformation doesn't come from institutional change or external force. It begins within—with love stirring our thoughts, reshaping our habits, and sending us outward as walking miracles. You are the vessel of divine disruption.

Final Invitation: Live the Reality

This isn't doctrine to debate—it's divine reality to embody. Any teaching that distracts from the success of the cross is a waste of time. The only possible way we delay the glory that follows the cross is by underestimating what happened when Jesus cried: "It is finished."

Galatians 2:20 — "I no longer live, but Christ lives in me."
John 15:4 — "Abide in Me, and I in you."
Ephesians 2:8–9 — "By grace you have been saved... not by works."
Romans 6:14 — "You are not under law, but under grace."
Romans 8:1–2 — "No condemnation... the Spirit has set you free."

The work is finished.
The reign has begun.
It is time for us to live in it, in Him.

Seeing others as God sees us —through the lens of Christ's love—is where heaven touches earth, one heart at a time. That's the essence of John 13:34: *"Love one another as I have loved you."* Not just affection, but love that restores, confronts, heals, and liberates.

Stripping away dogma to focus on what Jesus *actually did* invites a revolution of grace. The cross wasn't just successful—it was cosmic, shaking every system that thrives on shame, hierarchy, and fear. If His government is peace and His throne is love, then His kingdom must be embodied, not awaited.

This charts a true course for humanity - not just for reform, but renewal.

The work is finished. The kingdom is here. The invitation is simple yet profound: *Live as if it's true.* Let love define your theology, your politics, your priorities. Let restoration guide your activism. Let your life become a living declaration:
Christ is King, and His reign begins in me.

A Manifesto for the Finished Gospel

We declare that Jesus Christ has fulfilled His mission.

His life, death, burial, resurrection, ascension, enthronement, and the giving of the Holy Spirit at Pentecost mark the final and complete unveiling of God's plan for humanity.

"It is finished" was not a whisper of relief but a trumpet of victory.

The cross did not defer glory—it revealed it. Love did not lose to wrath—it triumphed over every distortion. In Christ, judgment has been poured out as mercy, and righteousness has been gifted—not earned.

The kingdom is now.

Not delayed, not political, but active—through restored hearts, reconciled relationships, and Spirit-filled lives. The Church is not waiting for a future reign; it is the living body of the King, radiating His glory and peace on earth.

Love is the government. Peace is the increase. Christ is the King.

We reject any teaching that postpones transformation. We denounce systems built on condemnation and control. We affirm that divine justice is restoration, and that the Spirit of Christ dwells among us to make all things new.

To underestimate the cross is to misrepresent the gospel.

We will see others as God sees us: fully redeemed, deeply loved, and divinely empowered. One person at a time, one act of grace at a time, we will embody the unstoppable, world-changing love of Christ.

This is the gospel. This is the revolution. It cannot be delayed. It will not be denied.

Foundation 1:
The Love That Fueled It All

Series: *The Finished Work of Christ: Establishing His Kingdom Within*
Theme: From Eternity Past to the Resurrection Present—Love Has Always Been Enough

---

Introduction: Before There Was Action—There Was Affection

Let us begin not in Eden, not at Sinai, not in Bethlehem—but before the foundations of the world. Paul declares in *Ephesians 1:4*:

"For He chose us in Him before the foundation of the world, to be holy and blameless in His sight—in love."

Love is not God's response to sin. Love is His eternal nature.
Before the serpent hissed, before Adam reached, before Israel wandered—God loved.
That love was never reactive—it was always redemptive.

This foundation is not about a doctrine. It's about a Person.
A Father who loved, a Son who embodied, a Spirit who indwells.
And this love has *never stopped pursuing*.

The Scriptural Heartbeat

- *John 3:16* — **Love gave** the only Son—not to appease, but to reconcile.

- *Romans 5:8* — **Love demonstrated** itself while we were at our worst.

- *Ephesians 2:4–5* — **Because of His great love... He made us alive with Christ.**

- *2 Corinthians 5:14* — **Love compels**—not law, not fear, not performance.

And again, in *Romans 8:38–39*:

"Nothing will be able to separate us from the love of God that is in Christ Jesus our Lord."

This is the love that fueled every footstep of Jesus' life: His inclusion, His forgiveness, His rebuke of religious arrogance, His death and resurrection.

The Curse vs The Cure: Redeeming Humanity from the Law

Religion tried to bind us under the curse of the law: External holiness. Transactional sacrifice. Hierarchical control. But *Galatians 3:13* says:

"Christ redeemed us from the curse of the law by becoming a curse for us..."

Let us be clear: God did not send Jesus to uphold religion. He sent Jesus to fulfill it—then transcend it with something deeper: *love incarnate*.

Romans 10:4 —

"Christ is the end of the law for righteousness to everyone who believes."

Love vs. Religion: A Clash of Kingdoms

Here we contrast what Jesus brought versus what religion offers:

Love	Religion
Internal transformation	External behavior modification
Identity by grace	Identity through performance
Relationship	Transaction
Dignity for all	Hierarchy of worth
Spirit-led freedom	Fear-based compliance
Eternal blueprint	Temporary scaffolding
Heirs and indwelt	Beggars and bound

Jesus didn't die to improve religion.

He died to **end the need for it**.

What Love Does

- Gives freely **without condition**
- Pursues relentlessly **without threat**
- Empowers change **without coercion**
- Restores dignity **without hierarchy**

- **Never fails, never ends, never loses**

This isn't theory. This is the **structure** of redemption.
Love isn't the background—it's the blueprint.
The finished work of Christ is what love looks like when it's not withheld.

Call to Personal Reflection

If love is the blueprint... have we let it rebuild us?

Ask:

- Do I still try to earn what was freely given?

- Do I cling to shame that love already silenced?

- Do I define myself by what religion demanded, or by what love declared?

Let us not preach a gospel that begins with guilt and ends in obligation. Let us preach—and live—a gospel that begins with love and ends in restoration.

The Open Door: From Love to Life

Ephesians 3:17–19 declares:

"I pray that you... being rooted and established in love, may have power... to grasp how wide and long and high and deep is the love of Christ... and to know this love that surpasses knowledge—that you may be filled to the measure of all the fullness of God."

Fullness is not found in knowledge—it is found in love.
The law excluded us.
Religion exhausted us.
Love indwells us.

And it wins.

Final Charge

This is not sentimental.
This is **structural**.
The love of God is the foundation stone of the finished work.
And if we build on any other foundation—performance, punishment, law—we build what God has already torn down.

Declaration

The love of God is my origin.
The love of Christ is my redemption.
The Spirit of love is my identity.
The reign of love is my reality.
And the finished work is my new beginning.

Foundation 2:

Not Just a Story A Revolution of Reality

Series: *The Finished Work of Christ: Establishing His Kingdom Within*
Theme: Christ Didn't Come to Start a Religion—He Came to End One and Begin a Kingdom

---

Opening Declaration

This is not mythology.
This is not parable or poetry.
This is the seismic announcement that heaven invaded earth and didn't ask religious approval to do it.

Jesus did not come to appease an angry Father.
He came to unveil Him as love incarnate.
He did not come to reclaim a throne—He never lost it.
He came to enthrone humanity inside divinity.

He didn't come to build temples with gates—
He tore every veil, broke every barrier, and moved the kingdom into **us**.

Scripture Foundation

- *John 17:4* — "I have glorified You on the earth. I have finished the work which You have given Me to do."

- *John 19:30* — "It is finished."

- *Hebrews 10:10* — "We have been sanctified through the offering of the body of Jesus Christ once for all."

Let those last three words ring like thunder:

Once.
For.
All.

The Kingdom Established—Not Reserved

The kingdom is not waiting.
It is not reserved for saints who "got it right."
It is not postponed until the smoke clears at the end of time.
It is **here**.
Now.
Inside.

You are not trying to get into it.
It is trying to get out of you.

This is the revolution of reality—
Not just a message to believe, but a reality to embody.
Jesus Christ established something **living**, not something liturgical.

Religion: The Imitation Gospel

Let's say it clearly:
Religion doesn't reveal God—it tries to contain Him.

Religion says...	Jesus demonstrates...
"You must appease God"	"I AM the full expression of the Father's heart"
"Obey to gain access"	"You carry access—you are the temple"
"Someday glory will come"	"Glory moved into you now"
"Sanctification is progressive"	"You are sanctified once for all"
"Jesus died to start Christianity"	"Jesus died to end separation and begin union"

Religion offers:

- Distance disguised as reverence

- Shame repackaged as humility

- Delay framed as discipleship

But what did Jesus say?

"The kingdom of God is **within you**" — *Luke 17:21*
He wasn't issuing hope—He was revealing reality.

A Gospel That Burns Down Distance

Religion builds altars.
Jesus became the final one.
Religion waits on heaven.

Jesus brought it near.
Religion says, "Try harder."
Jesus says, "It is finished."

The gospel is not a ladder to climb.
It's a floor to stand on—already built in the body of Jesus.

Hebrews 10:14 — "By one offering He has perfected forever those who are sanctified."

Theology of Revolution

Let us dismantle three pillars of religious dogma:

1. **Appeasement Theology** — the lie that God needed a blood payment to love us

Truth: Jesus was not changing God's heart toward humanity—He was revealing it.

2. **Progressive Access Doctrine** — the teaching that holiness increases over time

Truth: You have been made holy *once for all* (*Hebrews 10:10*)
Sanctification is not a staircase—it's a gift.

3. **Future Kingdom Concept** — the idea that heaven is distant or coming later

Truth: Christ is enthroned *now*. (*Ephesians 1:20–22*)
The kingdom is increasing through *us*.

Invitation to Live Inside the Revolution

You are not being recruited into a religion.
You are being awakened into a kingdom.
You are not joining a club—you are becoming a conduit.

Colossians 1:27 — "Christ in you, the hope of glory."

This revolution is internal, immediate, and irreversible.

Proclamation

Christ did not come to delay what love finished.
He did not come to decorate religion with mercy.
He came to destroy every barrier and build a home inside us.
What was finished then—is alive now.
And I am living proof.

Conclusion

You don't preach the gospel by retelling the story.
You preach it by announcing the revolution.
There is no veil.
There is no distance.
There is no delay.

The kingdom has come.
It is coming.
And it will keep coming—through **you**.

Foundation 3
His Life — The Revelation of the Father

Series: *The Finished Work of Christ: Establishing His Kingdom Within*
Theme: Jesus Didn't Come to Change God's Mind About Us—He Came to Show It Had Never Changed

---

Declaration

Jesus did not come to rescue us from the Father.
He came to introduce us to Him.
He didn't stand between us and wrath—He stood among us as love.
Not to pacify God's anger, but to unveil God's affection.

He came not as a diplomatic exception,
but as a radical example—of love, justice, and human dignity fully alive.

"If you've seen Me, you've seen the Father." — *John 14:9*

Religion Said: "God Is Angry"

Jesus Said: "He's Always Been Love"

Religion preaches separation:

- *God is holy—you are not.*

- *God is angry—you must appease Him.*

- *God is distant—you must chase Him.*

But Jesus walked the earth saying:

"I and the Father are one." — *John 10:30*
"The Father Himself loves you." — *John 16:27*
"Come to Me... I will give you rest." — *Matthew 11:28*

He did not soften a judgmental God—He shattered the misunderstanding of Him.
Christ didn't recalibrate the Father's mood. He **revealed His eternal heart.**

Scriptural Foundation

- *John 10:10* — "I came that they may have life, and have it abundantly."

- *Isaiah 53:3–5* — He bore our griefs, carried our sorrows. Not because wrath demanded it, but because **love insisted on healing.**

- *Luke 4:18–19* — Proclaiming liberty to the captives, recovery of sight, lifting the oppressed.

He moved through pain, not to prove divinity, but to elevate humanity.

His Life Was Divine Clarity in Human Form

What Jesus did wasn't just merciful—it was **subversive.**
He redefined access.
He rewrote worth.
He rebuilt belonging.

Here's what love accomplished through His life:

- He healed without conditions.

- He restored worth to the rejected.

- He called ordinary people into extraordinary purpose.

- He challenged religious gatekeeping and political power structures.

- He elevated the poor, the outcast, and the sinner to places of honor.

Love vs. Religious Dogma: A Direct Clash

Jesus' Life Declared	Religion Taught
God is accessible	God is restricted
Dignity is given	Worth must be earned
Holiness is healing	Holiness is separation
Ministry is restoration	Ministry is control
Justice lifts the broken	Judgment punishes the wounded
God touches lepers	God avoids the unclean

Religious dogma teaches divine distance.
Jesus teaches divine proximity.

The Fulfillment of the Law

He wasn't lawless—He was flawless.
His sinless life didn't merely obey the law—it **fulfilled it perfectly.**

"We do not have a high priest who cannot sympathize with our weaknesses... but one who was in all points tempted as we are, yet without sin." — *Hebrews 4:15*

His perfection wasn't cold compliance.
It was passionate love, embodied in truth.

And because He fulfilled the Law, He became the **Spotless Lamb**— qualifying to **abolish religion** and **establish kingdom.**

The Blueprint of Beloved Humanity

Jesus did not live above us. He lived *as us*, fully surrendered to divine presence.
He showed us not just what God is like—but what **we are meant to be**.

"Beloved children hosting divine presence."

You are not a failed version of humanity.
You are a home built for glory.
Jesus did not come to model unreachable perfection.
He came to reveal **redeemed identity**.

He wasn't showing off divinity.
He was showing us our destiny.

Call to Reflection

Ask your soul:

- Have I seen Jesus as God's revelation—or just God's apology?
- Am I trying to replicate holiness—or receive union?
- Do I preach a God who hides in temples—or One who dines with sinners?

Let His life expose every distorted belief.
Let His life elevate every buried dream.

Proclamation

I am not a sinner begging for access.
I am a child who bears the Father's likeness.
I do not preach religion.
I embody revelation.
Jesus showed me who I am.
And I will live like it's true.

Foundation 4:
His Death — Love's Ultimate Triumph

Series: *The Finished Work of Christ: Establishing His Kingdom Within*
Theme: The Cross Was Not Payment—It Was Restoration

Declaration

The cross was not a tragedy.
It was love's loudest triumph.
It did not rescue us from God—it reunited us with Him.
It was not wrath unleashed—it was mercy embodied.

Jesus didn't die *to make* salvation possible.
He died to declare it **finished.**
Not as a transaction—but as a transformation.

"God was in Christ reconciling the world to Himself." — *2 Corinthians 5:19*

Religion Said: "God Demands Payment"

Jesus Said: "Love Cancels the Debt"

Religion teaches appeasement:

- *Sacrifice, or suffer.*

- *Pay your debt, or perish.*

- *Blood buys forgiveness.*

But Jesus nailed every accusation to wood—not to satisfy vengeance, but to unleash reconciliation.

"He canceled the record of debt… nailing it to the cross." — *Colossians 2:14*
"Our old self was crucified with Him." — *Romans 6:6*

This wasn't divine punishment.
It was divine participation.
God did not abandon Jesus—God was **in** Him, undoing distortion with undying love.

Scriptural Foundation

- *John 12:32* — "When I am lifted up… I will draw all people to Myself."

- *John 19:30* — "It is finished."

- *Hebrews 9:12* — "He entered once for all… by means of His own blood."

- *Colossians 1:20* — Peace was made by the blood—not as appeasement, but as **embrace.**

- *1 Peter 3:18* — "Christ suffered once for sins… to bring us to God."

- *Romans 6:10* — "He died to sin once for all."

The cross didn't demand blood.
The cross poured love.

What He Accomplished

Let's declare it clearly:

- Fulfilled the Old Covenant sacrificial system

- Removed all barriers between God and humanity

- Reconciled all things through mercy, not wrath

- Declared the end of condemnation and the beginning of divine embrace

His death dismantled separation.
No curtain remains. No distance is left.
He turned crucifixion into coronation.

Mercy vs. Transaction: Reframing the Cross

What Religion Says	What Jesus Revealed
Blood satisfies God's anger	Blood demonstrates God's mercy
Sin separates us from God	Love reclaims us from distortion
Sacrifice buys forgiveness	Sacrifice declares forgiveness
Cross equals punishment	Cross equals participation
Salvation is future and conditional	Salvation is finished and present

He didn't die to uphold a divine ledger.
He died to erase it.

Insight: The Once-For-All Act

"After He had offered one sacrifice for sins forever, He sat down..." —
Hebrews 10:12

The altar is closed.
The curtain is torn.
The echo now resounds: **"Mercy remains."**

Judgment had its moment.
Love claimed eternity.

Jesus absorbed the distortion of empire, hierarchy, and shame.
And He didn't retaliate—He resurrected.
This wasn't divine vengeance—it was **divine vindication.**

A Kingdom-Driven Humanity

The cry *"It is finished"* was not a closing statement—it was a
commissioning.
What died in Him was distortion.
What rose with Him was divine possibility.

You are not awaiting salvation.
You are **living it.**
The kingdom is not delayed.
It has begun—with you.

Jesus didn't die to guilt humanity into worship.

He died to invite us into **union, identity, and purpose.**

Call to Reflection

Ask your soul:

- Am I still living like forgiveness is pending?

- Do I see the cross as wrath appeased—or mercy outpoured?

- Have I allowed religious distortion to frame divine reconciliation?

It is time to retire fear-based theology and rise into love-fueled identity.

Proclamation

I do not worship a God of wrath.
I worship a God revealed in Christ.
The cross did not separate—it united.
The blood did not buy love—it **revealed** it.
Jesus finished what religion cannot.
And I will live like it is true.

Conclusion

What religion complicated, Jesus completed.
What empire distorted, Jesus restored.
What shame buried, love resurrected.

He died once—for all.
And what remains is not wrath—it is **mercy, union, and commissioning.**

Humanity did not lose that day.
Humanity was crowned.

Foundation 5: His Resurrection — Reality Rewritten

Series: *The Finished Work of Christ: Establishing His Kingdom Within*
Theme: The Empty Tomb Was Not Symbolic — It Was Seismic

Declaration

The stone wasn't just rolled away—**reality was rewritten.**
The resurrection wasn't a reversal—it was a re-creation.
Death didn't lose politely—it was **dethroned, disarmed, and publicly disgraced.**

Jesus did not rise to prove a point—He rose to proclaim a new world.
What came out of that tomb was more than flesh restored.
It was humanity reborn, fearless and free.

"Christ, being raised from the dead, will never die again; death no longer has dominion over Him." — *Romans 6:9*

Religion Said: "Someday You'll Rise"

Jesus Said: "You're Alive Now"

Religion delays:

- *Someday you'll be forgiven.*

- *Someday you'll be free.*

- *Someday you'll overcome.*

But Jesus didn't rise for postponement—He rose for *empowerment.*

"As in Adam all die, so in Christ all will be made alive." — *1 Corinthians 15:22*
"He was delivered for our offenses and raised for our justification." — *Romans 4:25*

His resurrection is not a theological footnote.
It is the **validation** of the redemptive revolution.

Scriptural Foundation

- *Acts 13:38–39* — "Through Him everyone who believes is freed from all things."

- *Colossians 2:15* — He disarmed the powers, exposed their fraud, and triumphed openly.

- *Hebrews 2:14* — He destroyed death by entering it—and broke its ruler's grip.

- *1 Corinthians 15:17* — "If Christ has not been raised, your faith is futile..."

But He *has* been raised—so your faith is fierce.

What He Did After Rising

This wasn't myth or metaphor—it was movement:

- He appeared to hundreds

- He ate, walked, and spoke as fully alive

- He commissioned His followers with authority, not fear

- He broke the claim of darkness over humanity

- He crushed the power of accusation, shame, and fear

- He unveiled a kingdom that no longer negotiates with death

The resurrection isn't something we believe in—it's something we belong to.

Resurrection vs. Religious Delay

Religion Offers	Resurrection Declares
Future forgiveness	Present freedom
Future power	Present authority
Future transformation	Present participation
Spiritual hierarchy	Shared resurrection glory
Shame-based identity	Reborn image of God

You are not just saved—you are **raised.**
You are not just justified—you are **commissioned.**

Insight: Humanity Reborn

"If Christ is not raised... you are still in your sins." — *1 Corinthians 15:17*

But He rose—and sin lost its grip.

He rose—and shame lost its voice.
He rose—and we stepped into **new creation.**

His resurrection redefined what it means to be human:

- Not bound by sin

- Not intimidated by spiritual powers

- Not trapped in religious gatekeeping

We are not Adam's echo—we are Christ's image.

A Kingdom That Doesn't Bow to Death

This kingdom does not accommodate decay.
It does not negotiate with darkness.
It does not tolerate hierarchy or fear.

Jesus rose to **reframe reality**:
A people no longer defined by failure,
But by fullness.

Your resurrection is not pending—it is *present.*
You are living proof that love rewrites the final word.

Call to Reflection

Ask your soul:

- Do I live like resurrection has already happened?

- Am I reborn—or just rebranded?

- Have I allowed resurrection reality to reshape my dignity, power, and purpose?

It's time to move from belief to embodiment.

Proclamation

I am not waiting for freedom.
I am walking in it.
I do not fear death.
I carry resurrection.
Shame no longer names me.
Love has remade me.
The tomb is empty.
And so is my fear.

Conclusion

His resurrection was not symbolic—it was **seismic.**
It collapsed shame.
It crushed hierarchy.
It inaugurated a kingdom.

Christ did not rise alone—**He raised humanity with Him.**

Welcome to reality rewritten.
Welcome to resurrection.

Foundation 6: His Ascension — Heaven Touches Earth

Series: *The Finished Work of Christ: Establishing His Kingdom Within*
Theme: He Didn't Leave Us — He Relocated Authority

Declaration

Jesus didn't disappear.
He ascended—not to create distance, but to **disperse dominion**.
His departure wasn't abandonment.
It was **enthronement**.

The religious spirit laments that "Jesus left."
But the kingdom shouts, "He *reigns from within*."

"All authority... has been given to Me." — *Matthew 28:18*
"He was taken up before their eyes." — *Acts 1:9*

But what religion misses is this:
Jesus didn't leave to reign far away.
He ascended to **fill all things—especially us.**

Religion vs. Ascension Truth

Religion says:

- God is "up there" and we are "down here"

- Jesus left so we could long for return

- Heaven is distant and reserved

Ascension declares:

- Jesus reigns *in us*, not above us

- Heaven relocated to the human spirit

- Authority was distributed, not withheld

"He ascended... to fill all things." — *Ephesians 4:10*

Scriptural Foundation

- *Hebrews 1:3* — "He sat down at the right hand of the Majesty on high."

- *Hebrews 7:25* — "He always lives to make intercession for them."

- *Acts 1:9* — A visible departure that signaled invisible empowerment

Here's what this means:
Jesus did not escape history.
He **interrupted** it.
And now, seated in victory, He speaks through His body—*us*.

Insight: Enthronement, Not Absence

Jesus didn't ascend to detach.
He ascended to **distribute divine authority** into human vessels.

His throne is not an escape hatch.
It's the epicenter of heaven's expansion.

Religion preaches divine withdrawal.
The gospel preaches divine **infusion**.

The Ascension was the coronation of Christ,
and the commissioning of humanity.

He exchanged proximity for **permanence**.

Heaven Flows Through Humanity

This is the scandal of the Ascension:
Heaven now flows through **you**, not a temple.
Authority now operates through **spirit**, not system.
Jesus isn't reigning from behind a curtain—He's reigning through *flesh redeemed.*

Religion vs. Kingdom: Authority Disrupted

Religion Teaches	Ascension Reveals
God is absent, Jesus left	God is present, Jesus reigns in us
Wait for heaven	Release heaven now
Authority is for clergy only	Authority is for every believer
Intercession comes from men	Intercession comes through Christ alone

| Power flows from structure | Power flows from Spirit-indwelt saints |

He did not rise to leave us behind—He ascended to launch us forward.

What Ascension Accomplished

Let's name it clearly:

- Fulfilled the earthly mission

- Initiated heavenly intercession

- Seated humanity inside divine authority

- Signaled the start of a Spirit-filled age

- Dismantled dependence on institutional religion

- Entrusted the reign of heaven to a kingdom of priests

Heaven's throne didn't retreat—**it expanded.**

Call to Reflection

Ask your soul:

- Have I treated Ascension as distance, or distribution?

- Am I living as one sent in authority—or longing for proximity that was already given?

- Do I look to systems—or embrace indwelling reign?

You were never meant to be a spectator.
You are a participant—enthroned with Christ (*Ephesians 2:6*).

Proclamation

I do not chase a distant Jesus.
I carry a reigning King.
I do not wait for heaven to come.
Heaven has come into me.
I live from divine authority.
I move in permanent presence.
And I reveal the reign of Christ.

Conclusion

The Ascension isn't a farewell—it's a **framework**.
It restructured authority.
It relocated divinity.
It removed dependency on holy places and installed holy people.

The church isn't an institution waiting for revival.
The church is a kingdom carrying resurrection and reigning **now**.

Jesus ascended.
Humanity was enthroned.
And heaven touched earth—through *you*.

Foundation 7: His Enthronement — The Reign Has Begun

Series: *The Finished Work of Christ: Establishing His Kingdom Within*
Theme: The Throne Is Occupied. The King Reigns Now.

Proclamation

Jesus is not waiting.
He's not pacing the courts of heaven for a final trumpet.
He is enthroned—**now.**
The work is done. The reign has begun.

"He sat down at the right hand of God." — *Hebrews 10:12*
"Sit at My right hand..." — *Psalm 110:1*

Religion teaches delayed dominion.
But kingdom truth declares: **Authority is active. Power is present. Reign is real.**

Heaven's Perspective vs. Earth's Tradition

Let's confront it.

Tradition says:

- The throne is symbolic

- Christ's reign will come *later*

- Power is restrained until end times

- The gospel is transactional

Truth says:

- The throne is occupied

- The reign of Christ is *current*

- Power is flowing through Spirit-filled lives

- The gospel is transformational

"He is far above all rule and authority… for the church." — *Ephesians 1:20–22*

Insight: His Seat Means It's Finished

Jesus sat down because there's no more striving.
No more earning.
No more waiting for a better covenant.
This *is* the government.
And of His government and peace—*there will be no end* (Isaiah 9:7).

He isn't seated in delay.
He is seated in **dominion**.

The Coronation Has Already Happened

This isn't a rehearsal—it's a revolution.
Jesus isn't waiting to be crowned.
He was crowned when He overcame death, tore the veil, ascended on high, and **sat down.**

His throne is not ceremonial—it's operational.
And His reign is not distant—it's **within you.**

Reign Through Love, Not Control

His kingdom is unlike all others.
It doesn't conquer through coercion—
It transforms through **love**, **justice**, and **restoration**.

Earthly Kingdoms Reign By	Jesus' Kingdom Reigns By
Force and fear	Love and peace
Titles and positions	Spirit and adoption
Distance from the people	Indwelling the people
Laws imposed externally	Life manifested internally

Sons and Daughters Manifest the Kingdom

He reigns through **Spirit-filled sons and daughters**:

- Who reveal divine will in their everyday lives

- Who carry restoration into broken systems

- Who walk in peace without compromise

- Who live from victory, not for it

You're not waiting to become royalty.
You're walking in it.

The throne is full.
The Kingdom is moving.
And you are its vessel.

Built for Reign, Not Retreat

Ask yourself:

- Have I treated the throne as symbolic—or sovereign?

- Am I living from the finished work—or still striving?

- Does my life express restoration—or cling to control?

The reign of Christ isn't postponed.
It's **planted** in you.

"He has made us kings and priests to His God and Father." — *Revelation 1:6*

Proclamation

I do not wait for power—I walk in it.
I do not beg for presence—I bear it.
I do not fear the future—I manifest the kingdom now.
I reign through love.
I restore through justice.
I reveal heaven through who I am.

Conclusion

His enthronement was not a pause.

It was the unleashing of His reign through humanity.

He governs from within—not above.

And you are learning and helping to restore the gospel that says:

The throne is not reserved—**it is occupied.**

The reign is not coming—**it has begun.**

The King does not demand submission—**He instills love.**

This is not hope deferred—this is hope distributed.

Foundation 8: The Sending of the Spirit - The Indwelling of Jesus

Series: *The Finished Work of Christ: Establishing His Kingdom Within*
Theme: Pentecost Is Not a Religious Moment—It Is Divine Indwelling

---

Declaration

Pentecost was not God starting a new religion.
It was God **taking residence.**
Jesus didn't send *power*—He sent **Presence.**

"I will not leave you as orphans; I will come to you." — *John 14:18*
"He dwells with you and will be in you." — *John 14:16–17*

This was not substitution.
This was **continuation.**
Not visitation—**inhabitation.**

From Transaction to Transformation

The old covenant transacted with externals:

- Stone laws

- Holy buildings

- Hierarchical systems

The Spirit redefined everything:

- The law now written on **hearts**

- The temple now made of **flesh**

- The kingdom now flowing through **sons and daughters**

"Your body is a temple of the Holy Spirit." — *1 Corinthians 6:19*
"If Christ is in you... the Spirit gives life." — *Romans 8:9–11*

Pentecost: The Fulfillment of Promise

What happened was not random—it was **revelation**.

- Jesus **ascended** — to multiply His presence

- The Spirit **descended** — to indwell humanity

- Peter declared: "This is that" — *Acts 2:16–17*

- Wind and fire didn't symbolize religion—they **signaled release**

This wasn't a church service—it was a **cosmic shift**.

Old System vs. New Reality

Old Covenant System	Spirit-Filled Reality
External obedience	Internal transformation
Limited access (priests, prophets)	Universal access (sons, daughters)
Law on tablets	Law on hearts
Temporary visits	Permanent dwelling

Human mediation	Divine habitation

The Spirit doesn't visit believers—it **rebirths** them.

Insight: The Spirit Is Not a Feeling—It's a Person

The Spirit is not emotional hype.
The Spirit is not a vague force.
The Spirit is **Jesus in Spirit-form**, fulfilling His own promise.

"God sent the Spirit of His Son into our hearts..." — *Galatians 4:6*
"...crying, 'Abba, Father!'" — *Romans 8:15*

You don't access the Spirit through ritual.
You live in the Spirit through **relationship**.

What Pentecost Actually Did

Pentecost was:

- A transfer of divine location—from a heavenly throne to a human heart

- The democratization of kingdom power

- The internal witness of adoption

- The activation of divine life in ordinary people

- The beginning of Spirit-led existence—not Spirit-assisted religion

"This is the covenant I will make... I will put My law in their minds and write it on their hearts." — *Jeremiah 31:33*

Jesus Made Room—Then Filled It

He didn't just remove sin to secure forgiveness.
He removed sin to **make room**—for Himself.

The cross was the cleansing.
Pentecost was the **inhabiting.**

The Spirit is not an accessory to salvation.
It is the **proof** of salvation.

Proclamation

I am not waiting for God—I host Him.
I am not seeking a feeling—I carry a Person.
I am not a religious spectator—I am the dwelling place of Christ.
Pentecost was not a moment—it was my **birthright.**
Jesus didn't leave me behind—He came within me.

Conclusion

Pentecost isn't the origin of an institution.
It's the eruption of indwelling incarnation.
The Spirit doesn't speak from platforms—He speaks from people.
And now, **you are the place heaven touches earth.**
Jesus ascended. The Spirit descended. And now, the gospel *indwells*.

Foundation 9: Who We Became —
Spirit-Born Identity

Series: *The Finished Work of Christ: Establishing His Kingdom Within*
Theme: Pentecost Didn't Change the Atmosphere—It Changed Us

Proclamation

The goal of Pentecost wasn't behavior modification.
It was **identity transformation**.

Religion upgrades effort.
The Spirit **recreates essence**.

"Because you are sons, God sent the Spirit of His Son into our hearts..." — *Galatians 4:6–7*
"You are no longer a slave, but a son." — *Galatians 4:7*

We were not improved.
We were **reborn.**

What Religion Robbed

Religion told us:

- You're forgiven, but still filthy

- You're accepted, but barely

- You're saved, but weak

- You're loved, but at a distance

The Spirit reveals:

- You are **indwelt**
- You are **recreated**
- You are **sealed**
- You are **family**

"If anyone is in Christ, he is a new creation..." — *2 Corinthians 5:17*

The Identity Transfer

Before Pentecost	After Pentecost
Outsiders begging for favor	Sons indwelt with glory
Religious effort	Spirit empowerment
Law-bound behavior	Spirit-led identity
Visiting the divine	Hosting the divine
Bound by flesh	Reborn by Spirit

You were not made better. You were made *new.*

Who We Became

Let's name it clearly:

- **Temples of divine presence** — hosting heaven, not chasing it

- **Adopted heirs** — not tolerated, but treasured

- **New creations** — reborn, not remodeled

- **Ambassadors of heaven** — carriers of divine will

- **Unified body** — many parts, one Spirit, one mission

- **Living witnesses** — our lives echo resurrection power

"You are a chosen people, a royal priesthood..." — *1 Peter 2:9*

"You were marked... with a seal... guaranteeing our inheritance." — *Ephesians 1:13–14*

Insight: Indwelling Glory Redefines Us

The Spirit doesn't just **live in us**.
He **testifies through us.**
Your identity isn't shaped by your past.
It is shaped by the **presence within.**

Pentecost wasn't a performance—it was a **possession.**
The moment Christ moved **into humanity.**
Not to supervise. To **saturate.**

We are not sinners aspiring to sainthood.
We are **citizens of heaven**, born from above, carrying the government of restoration now.

Religion's View vs. Kingdom Reality

Religion Says	Spirit Reveals
You're a forgiven failure	You're a reborn son
You must strive to earn favor	You already host favor
You're still waiting to be made whole	You are a vessel of resurrection
The Spirit visits in moments	The Spirit inhabits forever

This isn't motivational theology.
This is **ontological transformation**.
Your identity is sourced from glory—not guilt.

Proclamation

I am not a sinner trying to perform.
I am a son reborn by Presence.
I do not strive to belong—I am sealed in inheritance.
I host Christ.
I echo resurrection.
I release heaven.
This is who I am—Spirit-born, glory-marked, loved without condition.

Conclusion

Pentecost didn't upgrade behavior—it redefined **being**.
It marked the shift from religion's striving to heaven's saturation.
You're not trying to become someone new.
You **are** someone new.

This is not spiritual enthusiasm.
It is eternal reality.
And you are the evidence.

Foundation 10: What This Means — Spirit-Shaped Mission and Community

Series: *The Finished Work of Christ: Establishing His Kingdom Within*
Theme: Pentecost Didn't Just Empower Individuals—It Reconfigured Reality

---

Declaration

The Spirit didn't land to stir emotions—
He came to **commission a people**.

Pentecost wasn't the birth of religion.
It was the beginning of a **new humanity**.
Not institution—but **incarnation**.
Not control—but **community**.
Not hierarchy—but **Spirit-led family**.

"We are one body in Christ..." — *Romans 12:4–5*
"To each is given the manifestation of the Spirit for the common good."
— *1 Corinthians 12:7*

Insight: The Spirit Reshaped the Mission

Pentecost did not create church culture.
It released **kingdom community**.

- Mission became **incarnational** — not outreach, but embodiment

- Love became **law** — not rules, but relational restoration

- Justice became **essential** — not optional activism, but divine mandate

- Healing became **normative** — not mystical moments, but ongoing life

- Church became **living** — not brick and mortar, but breath and movement

"Do justice, love mercy, walk humbly..." — *Micah 6:8*

Reconfigured Reality: Mission in Motion

Pentecost didn't just fill rooms with wind—
It filled the world with **witnesses**.

Religion's View of Church	Spirit's Definition of Church
Sunday gathering	Everyday embodiment
Clergy-led structure	Spirit-led body
Controlled access to ministry	Universal participation
Building-centered worship	Life-centered mission
Fear-based obedience	Love-based transformation

"The prayer of a righteous person is powerful..." — *James 5:16*

What This Means for Us

We are:

- **Temples on the move** — carrying presence into every space

- **Agents of healing** — releasing restoration where trauma ruled

- **Justice-bearers** — confronting oppression with mercy and truth

- **Sacred community** — every person is a priest, every table a sanctuary

- **Ecclesia redefined** — no more stage and spectators, only Spirit and sons

- **Love-driven people** — no longer ruled by law, but moved by compassion

---

Pentecost Replaced the Old Blueprint

Let's name what it ended and what it began.

Before Pentecost	After Pentecost
External religion	Internal regeneration
Hierarchical control	Holy Spirit-led unity
Divided roles	United function as one body
Cultural separation	Kingdom expression through all nations

Sacred places   Sacred people

This is no longer about **what you attend**.
It's about **what you become**.

The Church That Reveals Heaven

The Spirit-filled church is:

- A **body**, not a building

- A **family**, not a format

- A **mission**, not a monument

- A **river of love**, not a wall of rules

- A visible **expression of the invisible reign** of God

"They broke bread and lived in awe…" — *Acts 2:42–47*

Wherever the church goes, **heaven breaks in.**
Not through programs—through *people possessed by Presence.*

Proclamation

I do not just carry a message—I carry a kingdom.
I do not just attend a church—I am the church.
I do not just sing songs—I release healing.
I do not just preach justice—I embody it.
I do not wait for heaven—I reveal it.
The Spirit fills me.

Love leads me.
And the mission flows through me.

Conclusion

Pentecost is not a memory—
It is a **movement still unfolding**.

It didn't call us to gather in fear.
It launched us to walk in love.

You are a **Spirit-filled son**
In a **Spirit-shaped family**
On a **Spirit-defined mission**

Wherever you step—**reality shifts.**
Wherever you speak—**heaven echoes.**

Foundation 11: From Inside Us—Outward

Series: *The Finished Work of Christ: Establishing His Kingdom Within*
Theme: The Gospel Doesn't Just Speak—It Walks in Flesh

Declaration

The kingdom is not institutional.
It is **incarnational**.
It does not reside in cathedrals—it radiates from **carriers**.
You are not waiting to experience heaven.
You are its vessel.

"The kingdom of God is within you." — *Luke 17:21*
"Christ in you, the hope of glory." — *Colossians 1:27*

Everything Jesus finished was meant to be **experienced**, not **awaited**.
His work wasn't an invitation—it was a **release**.
The gospel is no longer just preached—it must be **embodied**.

What Religion Misunderstood

Let's name the distortion:

Religion teaches:

- Holiness as performance

- Ministry as hierarchy

- Access as occasional

- Change as external

- Glory as future

The gospel reveals:

- Holiness as identity

- Ministry as inheritance

- Access as indwelling

- Change as internal

- Glory as *present*

"Your body is a temple of the Holy Spirit." — *1 Corinthians 6:19*

This isn't mysticism.
This is **divine incarnation on human terms.**

Scriptural Framework

- *Luke 17:21* — The kingdom doesn't arrive with observation—it's **within**.

- *Colossians 1:27* — Christ in **you** is not a hope deferred—it's the hope revealed.

- *2 Corinthians 5:18* — "God... gave us the ministry of reconciliation."

- *Romans 6:4* — We now walk in **newness of life**—because **death is behind us.**

You're not just carrying a message—
You are walking as the **evidence** that heaven invaded humanity.

Who You Become

Through the finished work:

- **A living temple** — not a visitor to sacred spaces, but a sacred space yourself

- **A carrier of glory** — not chasing fire, but releasing it

- **An agent of reconciliation** — restoring what division fractured

- **A walking image of kingdom values**

    o **Love** over control

    o **Peace** over fear

    o **Dignity** over hierarchy

You are not just saved.

You are **commissioned as divine disruption** in a broken world.

From Institutional to Incarnational

Institutional Religion	Incarnational Kingdom
Buildings and schedules	Bodies and sacred rhythms
Events and liturgies	Embodied presence and love

Leadership by rank	Leadership by servanthood
Doctrinal control	Relational transformation
Transactional activity	Internal reality flowing outward

The old model asks:
"What does church look like?"
The kingdom asks:
"What does Jesus look like through *you*?"

Insight: The Gospel Walks in You

You are joined to Christ's death and resurrection—
Not by belief alone,
But by *incarnation*.

"We were buried with Him... and now walk in newness of life." — *Romans 6:4*

Transformation is not top-down.
It is *inside-out*.
It is **love reshaping thought**.
Presence rewriting habit.
Spirit redefining posture.

You are a vessel—
Not of theology alone,
But of **miracle made tangible.**

Proclamation

I do not wait for a building to worship.
I am the sanctuary.
I do not wait for ministry to begin.
I am the expression of reconciliation.
I do not search for glory.
I host it.
I am loved.
I am indwelt.
I am alive—because Jesus lives inside me.

Conclusion

You are not a churchgoer.
You are **Christ in motion**.
The resurrection wasn't just for Jesus.
It was for **you—to walk as a miracle in public**.

So let's retire institutional shadows.
And let divine image shine through real people—redeemed, radiant, relentless.

From inside us—**outward.**
From Spirit — **into space.**
From kingdom — **into culture.**

This gospel doesn't wait for permission.
It walks in flesh.
It wears your face.
And yes, it echoes your thunder.

Foundation 12 — Final Invitation: Live the Reality

Series: *The Finished Work of Christ: Establishing His Kingdom Within*
Theme: Heaven is not awaited. It is embodied.

Declaration

This isn't doctrine to debate—
It's divine **reality to embody**.
The cross doesn't need your defense—it needs your **incarnation**.

"It is finished." — *John 19:30*
Not a whisper of defeat, but a **cosmic shift**.
The systems of shame collapsed.
The reign of love began.

To delay glory is to **underestimate the cross**.
It was not symbolic.
It was **cataclysmic grace**.

Scriptural Framework

Verse	What It Establishes
Galatians 2:20	Christ lives in you—your ego is dethroned.
John 15:4	You are not distant—you are **woven into the vine**.
Ephesians 2:8–9	Grace, not effort, is the engine of salvation.

Romans 6:14	Law no longer reigns—**grace does.**
Romans 8:1–2	No condemnation. No chains. **Only Spirit and freedom.**
John 13:34	Love like Jesus. No exceptions, no qualifiers—just restoration.

Shaking the Systems

The cross didn't just save individuals.
It shattered every system based on:

- **Shame**

- **Hierarchy**

- **Fear**

- **Control**

If His throne is love,
And His government is peace—
Then the **kingdom is now,**
And **you are its living ambassador.**

Identity Redefined

You are not a believer who is waiting.
You are a **living declaration** of a finished kingdom.

You now walk as:

- **An embodiment of grace**

- **A mirror of divine love**

- **A freedom agent in bondage cultures**

- **A challenger of dogma, a liberator of truth**

- **A rebuke to shame-based religion**

- **A sanctuary in motion**

The work is done.

The reign has begun.

Your assignment? **Live as if it's true.**

The Call to Embody

This is not about proper theology.

It's about **gospel gravity** pulling heaven through you.

Let your:

- **Theology be shaped by love**

- **Politics be healed by reconciliation**

- **Activism be led by restoration**

- **Priorities be governed by kingdom presence**

"Love one another as I have loved you." — *John 13:34*

Love that **restores.**

Love that **confronts.**

Love that **heals.**

Love that **liberates**.

You don't just live under this love—
You **manifest it**.

Proclamation

I am not under law—
I am under grace.
I am not under condemnation—
I am under the Spirit.
I am not waiting for a throne—
I host it.
I am not debating doctrine—
I am demonstrating reality.
Christ is King,
And **His reign begins in me**.

Conclusion

This isn't the end.
It's the beginning of a people who don't wait for heaven,
But **live it**.
A people who don't defend the cross, But **unleash its success**.
Let the old institutions tremble.
Let the living temples rise.

The kingdom is not coming. It has come.
And it has your name on it.

"Church Is Not a Place"

The Subversive Truth That Got Stephen Stoned

Stephen's final sermon wasn't a theological misstep—it was a prophetic dismantling. He dared to say what I have been saying for decades: *"The Most High does not dwell in houses made by human hands."* (Acts 7:48)

That wasn't just a critique of the temple—it was a confrontation of the entire religious system.

And it cost him his life.

Why? Because when you declare that God's house is not down the street, you're not just relocating God—you're *liberating* Him. You're tearing down the walls that men built to contain Him, control Him, and monetize Him.

You're saying:

- God is not in the building. He's in the *body*.

- Church is not a destination. It's a *manifestation*.

- The temple veil wasn't just torn—it was *abolished*.

- Wherever you go – There church (Spirit of the Living Christ) *is*.

This is the kind of truth that doesn't just get you funny looks. It gets you *stoned*—by systems that fear freedom.

The Bible is a Kingdom Love Story

The Bible is not a rulebook, not a religion manual, not a mythological scrapbook. It's a royal saga. A passionate love story with a throne at its center. Unfortunately, some worship books and ignore the Living Spirit. That's the tragedy of bibliolatry—where the text becomes a substitute for the Voice. Where the version becomes king, and the King becomes a footnote. Let's break it down:

1. Love

The initiating force. The eternal nature of God. Love creates, pursues, suffers, and restores. It is not a concept—it is the *character* of the King.

2. A King

Not a distant deity, but a present ruler. Jesus is not waiting to reign—He *is* reigning. His kingdom is not coming—it *has come*. He rules not by coercion, but by communion.

3. A Royal Family

We are not subjects—we are *sons and daughters*. Not servants in the outer courts, but heirs seated with Christ. The gospel is not about adoption papers—it's about *bloodline restoration*.

4. An Inheritance

- **Given** in Eden: dominion, intimacy, co-creation.

- **Lost** through deception: shame, separation, hierarchy.

- **Restored** through Christ: union, authority, glory.

This is the arc. This is the story. This is the *gospel.* And it's not about going to heaven. It's about *heaven coming to us*—and staying.

The Royal Gospel: Love, King, Family, Inheritance — And the House That Cannot Be Built with Human Hands

The gospel is not a religion.
It is not a transaction.
It is not a threat.
It is a royal proclamation—a divine unveiling of who God is, who we are, and what has always belonged to us.

This is the story Scripture tells when read through the lens of the Finished Work. Not a tale of escape, but a drama of enthronement. Not a manual for morality, but a manifesto of *royalty*. Not a summons to a building, but an awakening to *being*.

Let us unveil the five pillars of the Royal Gospel.

---

1. Love — The Nature of the King

Before there was creation, there was communion. *(John 17:24)*
Before there was law, there was love. *(1 John 4:8)*
Before there was sin, there was *Sonship. (Ephesians 1:4–5)*

Love is not God's mood—it is His *nature. (1 John 4:16)*
It is the initiating force behind every movement of redemption.

- Love created us in His image. *(Genesis 1:26–27)*

91

- Love pursued us through our wandering. *(Luke 15:4–7)*

- Love absorbed our shame and restored our dignity. *(Hebrews 12:2; Isaiah 61:7)*

- Love reigns—not with fear, but with freedom. *(1 John 4:18; Galatians 5:1)*

This gospel begins and ends with love.
Not as sentiment, but as *substance*.
Not as emotion, but as *essence*.
Love is not the reward for obedience—it is the *origin of existence*. *(Jer31:3; Romans 5:8)*

---

2. A King — The Reigning Christ

Jesus is not waiting to be crowned. *(Hebrews 1:3; Revelation 1:5)*
He is not pacing heaven, hoping we'll behave.
He is enthroned—*now. (Ephesians 1:20–22)*
His kingdom is not delayed—it is *present. (Luke 17:21)*

He is the King who:

- Conquered death by surrender. *(Philippians 2:8–11; Hebrews 2:14)*

- Dismantled hierarchy by washing feet. *(John 13:3–5)*

- Reclaimed dominion by restoring identity. *(Romans 8:29–30; Revelation 5:10)*

He rules not by coercion, but by communion. *(John 15:4–5)*

Not by distance, but by *indwelling. (Colossians 1:27)*

Not by threat, but by *truth. (John 18:37; John 8:32)*

The gospel is not about earning His favor.

It is about *living from His reign. (Romans 5:17)*

We are not waiting for the kingdom to come—it has *already arrived,* because the King has already conquered. *(Colossians 2:15; Matthew 28:18)*

---

3. A Royal Family — Sons and Daughters, Not Subjects

We were never meant to be servants in the outer courts. *(John 15:15)*

We were born to be heirs in the throne room. *(Romans 8:16–17; Galatians 4:7)*

The gospel does not invite us to religion—it awakens us to *royalty.*

- We are not adopted into pity—we are restored into *position. (Ephesians 2:6; Romans 8:29)*

- We are not tolerated—we are *celebrated. (Luke 15:22–24)*

- We are not distant—we are *indwelt. (1 Corinthians 3:16; John 14:23)*

This family is not built on bloodlines or behavior.

It is built on *beloved identity. (Galatians 3:26–28)*

We are the image-bearers, the co-heirs, the living temples. *(Genesis 1:27; Romans 8:17; 1 Corinthians 6:19)*

The veil is torn. *(Matthew 27:51)*
The hierarchy is dismantled. *(Matthew 23:8–10)*
The family is restored. *(Ephesians 2:19–22)*

We are not members of an institution—we are *members of one another. (Romans 12:5)*
We are not attendees—we are *embodied presence. (2 Corinthians 6:16)*
We are not waiting to be accepted—we are *already home. (John 14:2–3; Colossians 3:3)*

---

4. An Inheritance — Given, Lost, Restored

The story of humanity is not one of failure—it is one of *reclamation.*

- **Given** in Eden: intimacy, authority, co-creation. *(Genesis 1:28; Genesis 2:15)*

- **Lost** through deception: shame, separation, striving. *(Genesis 3:7–10)*

- **Restored** through Christ: union, dignity, dominion. *(Rom 5:17; 2 Cor 5:17; Rev 1:6)*

The inheritance is not postponed—it is *present. (Ephesians 1:11; Colossians 1:12)*

We are not waiting to receive—we are awakening to what is already ours. *(2 Peter 1:3)*

This inheritance includes:

- The indwelling Spirit. *(Romans 8:9; John 14:17)*

- The mind of Christ. *(1 Corinthians 2:16)*

- The authority of love. *(John 13:34–35; 1 John 4:17)*

- The eternal now of divine presence. *(Hebrews 13:5; Matthew 28:20)*

We do not earn it. *(Titus 3:5)*
We do not qualify for it. *(Colossians 1:12)*
We *inherit* it—because we are *family. (Galatians 4:7)*

This is not a future reward—it is a *present reality.*
We are not spiritual beggars—we are *royal heirs. (Romans 8:17; Revelation 3:21)*

---

5. The House That Cannot Be Built — Church Reimagined

The gospel has been hijacked by buildings. *(Acts 7:48–49)*
The kingdom has been buried beneath programs.
The family has been fractured by hierarchy. *(1 Corinthians 1:12–13)*

But the truth remains:

Church is not a place. *(John 4:21–24)*

God's house is not down the street. *(Acts 17:24)*
You are the temple. *(1 Corinthians 3:16; Ephesians 2:22)*
We are the dwelling. *(2 Corinthians 6:16)*

The house of God is not made with hands—it is made with *hearts. (Hebrews 8:10)*
It is not constructed—it is *revealed. (Romans 8:19)*
It is not attended—it is *embodied. (Romans 12:1)*

Jesus did not die to fill pews.
He died to fill *people. (John 14:17; Galatians 2:20)*
He did not rise to start a service.
He rose to *restore a family. (Hebrews 2:11)*

The church is not a building you go to.
It is a *body you belong to. (1 Corinthians 12:27)*
It is not a Sunday event—it is a *daily reality. (Acts 2:46–47)*
It is not a hierarchy—it is a *household. (Ephesians 2:19)*

We are not called to build temples. *(Acts 17:24)*
We are called to *be them. (1 Peter 2:5)*
We are not summoned to sacred spaces.
We *are* the sacred space. *(1 Corinthians 6:19)*

This gospel does not call us to attend—it calls us to *awaken.*
(Ephesians 5:14)
To stop outsourcing presence.
To stop renting identity.
To stop confusing proximity with intimacy.

The Royal Gospel reclaims the church as a living, breathing, Spirit-filled family.
Not a brand.
Not a building.
Not a business.

But a *body. (Romans 12:5)*
A *bride. (Revelation 21:2)*
A *household of love. (1 John 4:12; Ephesians 3:17–19)*

The Royal Gospel Declared

This is the gospel:

- **Love as origin.** *(1 John 4:8; Jeremiah 31:3)*

- **Christ as King.** *(Revelation 1:5; Ephesians 1:20–22)*

- **Humanity as royal family.** *(Romans 8:16–17; Galatians 4:7)*

- **Inheritance as restored reality.** *(Ephesians 1:11; 2 Peter 1:3)*

- **Church as embodied presence.** *(1 Corinthians 3:16; Ephesians 2:22)*

It is not about going to heaven.
It is about heaven *inhabiting us. (Luke 17:21; Colossians 1:27)*
It is not about escaping earth.
It is about *redeeming it. (Romans 8:19–21)*

This gospel does not begin with sin—it begins with *Sonship.* *(Ephesians 1:4–5)*
It does not end with judgment—it ends with *joy. (John 15:11; Revelation 21:4)*
It does not demand fear—it invites *freedom. (Galatians 5:1; 2 Corinthians 3:17)*

You are not a sinner trying to behave.
You are a son or daughter learning to *believe. (John 1:12; Romans 8:14)*

This is the Royal Gospel.
And it is *already true. (John 19:30; Hebrews 10:14)*

The Great Distortion: An Indictment of Western Christianity

A System Built on Sand

What masquerades as Christianity in the West is, in large part, a religious industrial complex—an empire of dogma, hierarchy, and institutional self-preservation. It is not the gospel of Jesus Christ. It is a system built on fear, sustained by control, and perpetuated through theological distortion.

- **Heaven as Escape Hatch**: The dominant narrative teaches that the goal of life is to die well enough to earn heaven. This post-mortem obsession has gutted the gospel of its present power. Christ's reign is treated as a future fantasy, not a present reality.

- **Struggle as Virtue**: Suffering is romanticized, not as a consequence of a broken world but as a badge of spiritual merit. "Strive harder," they say. "Endure more." The cross becomes a tool of guilt rather than a declaration of victory.

- **Fear as Foundation**: Eternal torment is dangled like a sword over the heads of believers. The message is clear: conform or burn. This fear-based theology produces anxious, exhausted souls who never feel safe in the arms of God.

- **Hierarchy as Holiness**: Power structures mimic corporate ladders. Pastors become CEOs. Titles replace servanthood. The sacred is commodified, and access to God is mediated through human gatekeepers.

- **Dogma over Dignity**: The system demands allegiance to creeds and traditions, even when they contradict the character of Christ. Questioning is punished. Doubt is demonized. Conformity is rewarded.

- **Delayed Glory, Denied Empowerment**: The emphasis on "one day in glory" robs people of the truth that Christ's victory is now. The Spirit is sidelined. The believer is disempowered. The kingdom is postponed.

Cosmic Consequences

This distortion hasn't just wounded individuals—it has fractured the cosmos.

- **Creation Groans**: Identity distortion delays the unveiling of God's sons and daughters. Religion buries the true self beneath shame and striving. Creation is groaning for awakened image-bearers who live from the Finished Work.

- **Society Fractures**: Racism, patriarchy, nationalism, and economic exploitation are baptized in religious language. The church becomes complicit in systems of oppression, offering prayers instead of justice.

- **Mental Health Crisis**: Guilt, shame, and spiritual anxiety plague believers. The system teaches them to distrust their own worth, their own thoughts, even their own experience of God.

- **Division as Doctrine**: Denominations multiply like fractures in a broken bone. Unity is sacrificed on the altar of doctrinal purity. The Body of Christ is dismembered in the name of theological correctness.

- **Love Replaced by Law**: The extravagant love of God is buried beneath rules, rituals, and requirements. Grace is rationed. Mercy is conditional. The gospel becomes a transaction, not a transformation.

Theological Malpractice

Let's name the distortions for what they are:

Distortion	What It Claims	What It Actually Does
Penal Substitution as Sole Lens	God needed to punish Jesus to forgive us	Paints God as wrathful and transactional
Rapture Theology	Jesus will snatch believers away from a doomed world	Encourages escapism and neglect of justice

Distortion	What It Claims	What It Actually Does
Eternal Conscious Torment	Hell is God's eternal punishment for unbelievers	Instills fear, trauma, and spiritual paralysis
Clericalism	Only ordained leaders can rightly interpret Scripture	Disempowers the believer and creates dependency
Prosperity Gospel	Faith guarantees wealth and success	Exploits the poor and distorts suffering
Purity Culture	Holiness is tied to sexual behavior	Shames bodies and distorts identity
Nationalism	God favors certain nations or political ideologies	Hijacks the gospel for power and control

These are not harmless theological quirks. They are spiritual malpractice. They misrepresent the heart of God, distort the person of Christ, and sabotage the work of the Spirit.

The Explosion of Love: The Finished Work of Christ

The Finished Work of Christ is not a footnote to religious tradition. It is a cosmic detonation of love, freedom, and dignity. It dismantles every distortion and restores the gospel to its rightful glory.

- **Christ's Reign Is Now**: The resurrection wasn't a preview—it was a coronation. Jesus reigns now. The kingdom is here. Heaven is not a distant reward—it's a present reality breaking into the world.

- **Love Is the Law**: The only law that governs the kingdom is love. Not fear. Not hierarchy. Not performance. Love that dignifies. Love that liberates. Love that restores.

- **Freedom Is the Fruit**: The gospel sets people free—from guilt, shame, striving, and fear. It doesn't demand perfection. It declares completion. "It is finished" means there's nothing left to earn.

- **Dignity Is Restored**: Every human bears the image of God. No title, no institution, no doctrine can add or subtract from that truth. The gospel restores what religion tries to control.

- **Empowerment Is Immediate**: The Spirit is not reserved for the elite. Every believer is a temple. Every person is invited to participate in the divine dance of love and restoration.

- **Creation Is Included**: The gospel is cosmic. It's not just about souls—it's about soil. Christ's redemption touches every molecule of creation. The earth is not disposable—it's sacred.

How We Got Here: The Hijacking of the Royal Gospel

1. The Original Pulse — First and Second Century AD

The earliest followers of Jesus didn't build cathedrals—they *became* temples. They didn't form institutions—they formed *families*. The gospel they carried was not a religion—it was a revelation:

- Christ had reconciled the world. *(2 Corinthians 5:19)*

- The kingdom was present. *(Luke 17:21)*

- Love was the law. *(John 13:34)*

- All were included. *(Galatians 3:28)*

They gathered in homes, shared resources, healed the sick, and lived with radical joy and authenticity. Growth was organic. Leadership was relational. The Spirit was trusted.

But this movement was dangerous to empire. It couldn't be taxed, controlled, or weaponized. So, it was persecuted.

Yet it grew.

---

2. The Turning Point — Constantine and the Third Century Shift

By the early 3rd century, the kingdom message was proliferating. It was transforming lives, communities, and cultures. Then came

Constantine. In 312 AD, Constantine claimed victory in battle under the banner of Christ. He legalized Christianity, then institutionalized it. What had been a grassroots movement of love became a state-sanctioned religion of power.

This was the hijacking.

- The cross became a sword.

- Baptism became a badge of citizenship.

- Bishops became bureaucrats.

- The Church became an arm of empire.

The gospel was no longer proclaimed—it was *enforced*. The kingdom was no longer embodied—it was *branded*. And the message of reconciliation was buried beneath creeds, councils, and control.

---

3. The Rise of Dogma — Councils, Creeds, and Control

From the 4th to 6th centuries, a series of church councils codified doctrine—not to clarify truth, but to consolidate power. Disagreement was labeled heresy. Inclusion was replaced by orthodoxy. The Spirit's voice was replaced by imperial decree.

Key distortions emerged:

- **Original sin** replaced original blessing.

- **Hierarchy** replaced mutual honor.

- **Fear of hell** replaced assurance of love.

- **Clergy/laity divide** replaced shared priesthood. *(1 Peter 2:9)*

- **Sacraments** became gatekeepers instead of celebrations.

The Bible was chained to pulpits. The people were kept in ignorance. And the gospel became a tool of control.

---

4. Medieval Religion — Power, Penance, and Punishment

From the 7th to 15th centuries, the Church became a global institution. It amassed wealth, land, and armies. It sold indulgences, waged crusades, and silenced dissent. The message of Christ was buried beneath layers of ritual, fear, and superstition.

The kingdom was no longer a present reality—it was a distant reward.
God was no longer Abba—He was Judge.
Salvation was no longer a gift—it was a transaction.

This was not Christianity. It was *Christendom*.
A system built on fear, not love.
On hierarchy, not family.
On empire, not kingdom.

---

5. Reformation and Resistance — Partial Recovery

The 16th century brought reformers who challenged corruption. Luther, Calvin, and others reclaimed grace and Scripture. But even the Reformation was incomplete.

- It reformed doctrine, but not hierarchy.

- It reclaimed justification, but not inclusion.

- It emphasized faith, but still feared hell.

The Royal Gospel remained obscured. The Finished Work was still conditional. The Church remained divided, institutional, and often violent.

Yet throughout history, voices emerged—mystics, prophets, poets—who carried the flame. They spoke of union, love, and the indwelling Christ. They were often marginalized, but they kept the pulse alive.

---

6. Enlightenment and Modernity — Reason Over Revelation

The 18th and 19th centuries saw the rise of rationalism. Faith was reduced to moralism. Theology became academic. The Spirit was sidelined. The gospel was dissected, debated, and domesticated.

Church became a Sunday event.
Salvation became a personal escape plan.
The kingdom became a future hope.

And the Royal Gospel was buried beneath sermons, systems, and seminaries.

---

7. The Present Crisis — Fragmentation and Awakening

Today, we see the fruit of centuries of distortion:

- Churches divided by doctrine.

- Believers burned out by performance.

- Leaders trapped in hierarchy.

- The gospel reduced to sin management.

But the Spirit is stirring.

People are awakening to the Finished Work.
They are rediscovering the Royal Gospel.
They are reclaiming love, family, inheritance, and presence.

This is not a new movement.
It is a *return* to the original pulse.
It is the *Spirit correcting the course*.
It is the *kingdom reclaiming its voice*.

The Redemption of the Story

You asked how we got here. The answer is layered:

- Empire hijacked the gospel.

- Religion institutionalized it.

- Dogma distorted it.

- Fear weaponized it.

- But the Spirit never abandoned it.

Now, we redeem the story—not by rewriting history, but by *reclaiming truth*.
We don't fight the system—we *outgrow* it.
We don't shame the past—we *heal* it.
We don't wait for revival—we *live* it.

The Royal Gospel was never lost.

It was buried.

And now, it is *resurrecting*.

The distortion is layered like sediment, each era compacting another falsehood over the living truth. The next section will be called **"Echoes of the Hijack"**—where each distortion gets its own spotlight. Not to overwhelm, but to awaken. To show you that the Royal Gospel isn't fragile—it's indestructible. And it's rising again.

Echoes of the Hijack

Echo #1: Constantine's Imperial Adoption of Christianity

"The moment love was replaced by force, and the kingdom was co-opted by empire."

Where It Happened

- **Roman Empire**, 4th century AD
- Key events:
    - **Battle of the Milvian Bridge (312 AD)**
    - **Edict of Milan (313 AD)**
    - **Council of Nicaea (325 AD)**

Who Was Involved

- **Flavius Valerius Constantinus (Constantine the Great)**
    - Roman Emperor (306–337 AD)
    - Proclaimed Christianity as favored religion
    - Baptized on his deathbed by **Eusebius of Nicomedia**, an Arian bishop
- **Licinius** (co-emperor, later defeated)
- **Eusebius of Caesarea** (court historian and theological architect of imperial Christianity)

Driving Force Behind the Shift

- **Realpolitik**: Constantine saw Christianity as a unifying tool to consolidate power across a fractured empire

- **Vision before battle**: "In this sign, conquer" (Chi-Rho) became a symbol of divine endorsement for imperial conquest

- **Desire for control**: Christianity offered a structured, loyal base—ideal for imperial propaganda and social cohesion

What Was Hijacked

- **The Kingdom of God**:

  o Originally a nonviolent, relational, Spirit-led movement of love and mutuality

  o Transformed into a state religion with creeds, councils, and coercion

- **Ecclesia**:

  o Organic assemblies replaced by basilicas and hierarchical clergy

- **The Gospel**:

  o Reframed as allegiance to empire and orthodoxy, not liberation through love

- **Jesus' Way**:

  o The cross became a symbol of conquest, not self-giving love

The Distortion

- Christianity became **Christendom**—a fusion of throne and altar

- The **Constantinian Shift** birthed:

  o State-sponsored orthodoxy

  o Persecution of dissenters

  o The rise of imperial theology

  o The suppression of alternative expressions of faith

"One God, One Emperor, One Church" became the imperial slogan—obliterating the radical inclusivity and decentralization of the original movement

---

Echo #2: Replacement of *Ecclesia* with Institutional "Church"

"A living assembly turned into a static organization, severing relational roots."

Where It Happened

- **Post-Constantinian Roman Empire**, 4th century onward

- Key transitions:

  o **Council of Nicaea (325 AD)**: centralized authority

  o **Latin Vulgate translation (late 4th century)**: ecclesia rendered as "church"

- o **King James Bible (1611)**: institutional bias preserved the term "church" over "assembly"

Who Was Involved

- **Emperor Constantine**: laid the groundwork for ecclesial centralization

- **Eusebius of Caesarea**: promoted imperial theology

- **Jerome**: translated the Latin Vulgate, reinforcing institutional terminology

- **King James translators**: deliberately retained "church" to support Anglican structure

- **Roman Catholic hierarchy**: formalized the clergy system and sacramental control

Driving Force Behind the Shift

- **Control and Uniformity**:

  - o Empire needed a centralized religious structure to maintain order

  - o Bishops became imperial administrators

- **Translation Manipulation**:

  - o "Ecclesia" (Greek: *ekklēsía*, "called-out assembly") was replaced with "church" (from *kyriakon*, "belonging to the lord")—shifting focus from people to place

- **Architectural Shift**:

  - o Basilicas replaced homes; gatherings became services

      o   Buildings became symbols of power, not presence

What Was Hijacked

- **Relational Assembly:**

  o   *Ecclesia* was a Spirit-led, participatory community

  o   Replaced by hierarchical, clergy-led services

- **Mutual Indwelling:**

  o   Every believer was a priest; now only the ordained were "authorized"

- **Kingdom Functionality:**

  o   The ecclesia was meant to be a governing body of love and justice

  o   Reduced to ritual observance and institutional loyalty

The Distortion

- The word "church" became synonymous with **buildings**, **denominations**, and **authority structures**

- The **clergy-laity divide** was reinforced

- The **Spirit-led movement** was replaced by **programmatic religion**

- The **body of Christ** became a **brand**, not a living organism

"Jesus never said He would build a religion. He said He would build His *ecclesia*—a called-out people, not a called-in audience."

Echo #3: The Clergy-Laity Divide

"Hierarchy installed where mutual indwelling once reigned."

Where It Happened

- **Late 1st to 4th century AD**, intensifying post-Constantine

- Key transitions:

    o **End of 1st century**: emergence of formal leadership roles

    o **3rd–4th centuries**: clergy elevated as sacred class

    o **Medieval era**: full institutionalization of priesthood and sacramental control

Who Was Involved

- **Ignatius of Antioch** (c. 35–107 AD): early advocate of bishop-centered authority

- **Tertullian**, **Cyprian**, and later **Augustine**: reinforced clerical hierarchy

- **Roman bishops**: consolidated power, claiming apostolic succession

- **Medieval Church councils**: codified clerical privileges and sacramental gatekeeping

Driving Force Behind the Shift

- **Control and Sacralization:**

- o As Christianity grew, leaders sought to formalize roles to maintain order

- o Clergy were framed as intermediaries between God and people

- **Empire Influence**:

  - o Titles, robes, and rituals mirrored Roman governance

  - o The Church adopted imperial structures to legitimize authority

- **Fear and Illiteracy**:

  - o With Scripture inaccessible to most, clergy became sole interpreters of truth

What Was Hijacked

- **The Priesthood of All Believers** *(1 Peter 2:9)*:

  - o Every believer was meant to carry the Spirit and minister

  - o Replaced by a two-tier system: "called" vs. "common"

- **Mutuality and Shared Leadership** *(Ephesians 4:11–13; Romans 12:4–8)*:

  - o Gifts were meant to function in harmony

  - o Replaced by top-down control and passive spectatorship

- **Organic Worship and Community** *(Acts 2:42–47)*:

    o   Replaced by scripted liturgy and clerical performance

The Distortion

- The Church became a **spectator event**, not a participatory body

- Ministry became **professionalized**, not Spirit-led

- The laity were taught to **receive**, not to **reign**

- Clergy became **gatekeepers of grace**, rather than **equippers of saints**

"Jesus never ordained a priesthood. He called friends, brothers, and co-heirs. The early Church had leaders—but not overlords."

Echo #4: The Doctrine of Original Sin

"Inherited guilt where divine image once stood."

Where It Happened

- **Late 2nd to 5th century AD**, crystallized by Augustine of Hippo

- Key milestones:

    o   **Irenaeus** (c. 130–202): introduced inherited corruption

    o   **Augustine** (354–430): formalized "original sin" as transmitted guilt

    o   **Councils of Carthage & Orange**: codified the doctrine into orthodoxy

Who Was Involved

- **Augustine of Hippo:**
    - Claimed Adam's sin corrupted all humanity
    - Taught that guilt was biologically inherited through sexual reproduction

- **Pelagius:**
    - Opposed Augustine, affirming human freedom and innocence

- **Church Councils:**
    - Sided with Augustine, embedding inherited guilt into Christian identity

Driving Force Behind the Shift

- **Control through Shame:**
    - A theology of guilt made people dependent on institutional grace

- **Philosophical Influence:**
    - Augustine's Manichaean past shaped his view of the body as corrupt

- **Sacramental Gatekeeping:**
    - Baptism became the cure for congenital damnation

- **Empire Theology**:

  o A fallen humanity justified hierarchical mediation and divine monarchy

What Was Hijacked

- **The Image of God in Humanity** *(Genesis 1:26–27)*:

  o Replaced by a doctrine of depravity

- **Christ's Finished Work** *(Romans 5:18–19)*:

  o Overshadowed by inherited condemnation

- **Freedom and Responsibility** *(Ezekiel 18:20)*:

  o Replaced by ancestral guilt

- **Original Blessing** *(Genesis 1:28)*:

  o Rewritten as original curse

The Distortion

- Humanity was reframed as **born guilty**, not **born beloved**

- Salvation became **transactional**, not **transformational**

- The Gospel became **a rescue from wrath**, not **a revelation of union**

- The Church became **a dispenser of cleansing**, not **a witness to grace**

"Original Sin taught us to distrust our nature, fear our bodies, and beg for worth. But Christ came to reveal our belovedness, not to erase our origin."

Echo #5: Penal Substitution

"Wrath appeased where love was poured out."

Where It Happened

- **16th century Reformation**, formalized by **John Calvin**

- Key developments:

    o **Anselm of Canterbury** (11th century): introduced satisfaction theory

    o **Martin Luther & Calvin**: reframed it as legal punishment

    o **Reformed theology**: made it central to atonement doctrine

Who Was Involved

- **John Calvin**: taught that Christ bore God's wrath as our substitute

- **Charles Hodge** & **Wayne Grudem**: systematized it in modern theology

- **Evangelical tradition**: made it the dominant view of salvation

- **Critics**: from **Greg Boyd** to **Orthodox theologians**, have called it a distortion

Driving Force Behind the Shift

- **Legal Framework**:

    o   Sin was treated as a crime requiring punishment

    o   God's justice was framed as retributive, not restorative

- **Divine Wrath**:

    o   Jesus was seen as absorbing God's anger to satisfy justice

- **Sacrificial Logic**:

    o   Echoes of pagan appeasement rituals crept in

    o   The cross became a transaction, not a revelation

What Was Hijacked

- **The Nature of God** *(1 John 4:8)*:

    o   Love was subordinated to wrath

- **The Meaning of the Cross** *(Colossians 2:15; John 12:32)*:

    o   Victory and revelation replaced by punishment and appeasement

- **Union with Christ** *(Galatians 2:20)*:

    o   Replaced by substitution without transformation

- **Forgiveness** *(Luke 15; Matthew 18)*:

    o   Replaced by debt collection through blood

The Distortion

- God was portrayed as **needing violence** to forgive

- Jesus became **a scapegoat**, not a revealer of divine mercy

- The Gospel became **a courtroom drama**, not a love story

- The cross was reduced to **a payment**, not a proclamation

"The Father didn't punish the Son. He gave Himself in the Son. The cross wasn't divine vengeance—it was divine vulnerability."

Echo #6: Eternal Conscious Torment

"Endless agony where restoration was promised." This is one of the most haunting distortions ever canonized.

Where It Happened

- **4th to 6th century AD**, intensified in medieval theology

- Key milestones:

  - **Tertullian** (c. 160–220): introduced eternal punishment

  - **Augustine** (354–430): cemented it as orthodoxy

  - **Medieval sermons**: weaponized it to instill fear

  - **Reformation & Revivalism**: reinforced it through fiery preaching

Who Was Involved

- **Augustine of Hippo**: taught that hell was eternal conscious suffering

- **Thomas Aquinas**: argued the saved would rejoice in the torment of the damned

- **Jonathan Edwards**: preached vivid images of divine wrath and endless pain

- **Modern defenders**: cite Matthew 25:46 and Revelation 14:11 as proof texts

Driving Force Behind the Shift

- **Fear as Control**:

  - Eternal torment became a tool to enforce obedience

- **Empire Theology**:

  - Mirrored Roman justice—punishment without rehabilitation

- **Philosophical Dualism**:

  - The soul was seen as immortal, requiring an eternal fate

- **Misreading of Scripture**:

  - "Eternal" was interpreted as duration, not consequence or impact

What Was Hijacked

- **God's Restorative Justice** *(Isaiah 1:26; Acts 3:21)*:

    o Replaced by retributive vengeance

- **Christ's Victory Over Death** *(1 Corinthians 15:22–26)*:

    o Replaced by eternal separation

- **The Heart of the Father** *(Luke 15)*:

    o Replaced by judicial wrath

- **The Purpose of Judgment** *(John 3:17; Romans 2:4)*:

    o Replaced by final torment

The Distortion

- Hell became **a place of endless conscious suffering**, not a **metaphor for separation or consequence**

- God was portrayed as **inflicting infinite punishment for finite sins**

- The Gospel became **a rescue from torture**, not **a revelation of love**

- Evangelism became **fear-based**, not Spirit-led

"Jesus warned of Gehenna—a valley of burning trash, not an eternal torture chamber. He came to seek and save, not to condemn and torment."

Echo #7: Sacramental Gatekeeping

"Grace monopolized where communion once flowed." A piercing look at how the living Word was flattened into static ink.

Where It Happened

- **3rd to 13th century AD**, peaking in the medieval Church

- Key transitions:

    o **Cyprian of Carthage** (c. 200–258): "No salvation outside the Church"

    o **Council of Trent** (1545–1563): codified sacramental theology

    o **Medieval priesthood**: claimed exclusive authority over sacraments

Who Was Involved

- **Early bishops**: began asserting control over baptism and Eucharist

- **Medieval clergy**: elevated sacraments as channels of institutional grace

- **Church councils**: defined sacraments as necessary for salvation

- **Reformers**: challenged gatekeeping but often retained sacramental control

Driving Force Behind the Shift

- **Control of Access**:
    - Sacraments became tools to regulate inclusion and obedience

- **Institutional Power**:
    - The Church positioned itself as the sole mediator of divine grace

- **Fear of Heresy**:
    - Restricting communion was used to enforce doctrinal conformity

- **Empire Logic**:
    - Grace was no longer freely given—it was administered by hierarchy

What Was Hijacked

- **The Table of Fellowship** *(Luke 22:14–20; Acts 2:46)*:
    - Replaced by altar exclusivity and clerical mediation

- **The Spirit's Accessibility** *(John 4:23–24; 1 Corinthians 12:7)*:
    - Replaced by ritual dependency

- **The Body of Christ** *(1 Corinthians 10:17)*:
    - Fragmented into clergy vs. laity

- **The New Covenant** *(Hebrews 8:10–12)*:

    o   Replaced by institutional contracts

The Distortion

- Communion became **a privilege**, not a shared celebration

- Baptism became **a rite of entry**, not a sign of Spirit-filled belonging

- Grace was **administered**, not **embodied**

- The Church became **a dispenser of holiness**, not **a community of saints**

"Jesus broke bread with sinners, not gatekeepers. The early Church gathered in homes, not cathedrals. Grace was never meant to be rationed."

Echo #8: Biblical Literalism

"Text frozen where Spirit once breathed."

Where It Happened

- **Post-Reformation era**, intensifying in **19th–20th century fundamentalism**

- Key transitions:

    o   **Martin Luther**: elevated sola scriptura to counter corrupt hierarchy

- o **Charles Hodge & R.A. Torrey**: promoted inerrancy and literalism

- o **Modern Evangelicalism**: equated faithfulness with literal interpretation

Who Was Involved

- **Fundamentalist theologians**: codified literalism as orthodoxy

- **Dispensationalists**: read Scripture through rigid prophetic frameworks

- **Literalist pastors and apologists**: taught "God said it, I believe it, that settles it"

- **Critics**: like Michael Heiser and Matt Ayars, warned of flattening Scripture's dynamism

Driving Force Behind the Shift

- **Fear of Liberalism:**

    - o Literalism became a defense against modern skepticism

- **Desire for Certainty:**

    - o Scripture was treated as a rulebook, not a relational revelation

- **Control of Interpretation:**

    - o Literal readings reinforced doctrinal gatekeeping

- **Loss of Genre Awareness**:

    o   Poetry, parable, and apocalyptic were read as historical fact

What Was Hijacked

- **The Living Word** *(Hebrews 4:12; John 1:1)*:

    o   Replaced by static text divorced from Spirit

- **Prophetic Imagination** *(Isaiah 55:10–11; Revelation 21)*:

    o   Replaced by rigid timelines and fear-based eschatology

- **Poetic Revelation** *(Psalms, Song of Songs, Job)*:

    o   Reduced to literal propositions

- **Spirit-Led Interpretation** *(John 16:13; 2 Corinthians 3:6)*:

    o   Replaced by proof-texting and dogmatic systems

The Distortion

- Scripture became **a weapon**, not a wellspring

- Faith became **intellectual assent**, not relational trust

- The Bible was treated as **a flat map**, not a living landscape

- Literalism led to **absurd conclusions**—flat earth, geocentrism, and fear-based theology

"The Word was made flesh—not paper. Jesus interpreted Scripture with parables, questions, and Spirit-led insight. Literalism strips away the mystery and poetry of divine revelation."

Echo #9: End Times Obsession

"Escape glorified where incarnation once dwelled." Escapist theology has hijacked hope.

Where It Happened

- **19th–20th century**, fueled by **Dispensationalism** and **Revivalism**

- Key milestones:

  o **John Nelson Darby**: introduced pre-tribulation rapture theology

  o **C.I. Scofield**: popularized it through his annotated Bible

  o **Hal Lindsey & Tim LaHaye**: sensationalized it in books like *The Late Great Planet Earth* and *Left Behind*

Who Was Involved

- **Dispensationalist theologians**: divided history into rigid "ages"

- **Evangelical preachers**: used apocalyptic fear to drive conversions

- **Christian Zionists**: linked modern Israel to prophetic timelines

- **Media & pop culture**: reinforced escapism through films, fiction, and prophecy charts

Driving Force Behind the Shift

- **Fear-Based Evangelism:**

    o   Salvation became a ticket out of tribulation

- **Political Theology:**

    o   Prophecy was used to justify geopolitical agendas

- **Distraction from Justice:**

    o   Suffering was interpreted as "signs," not calls to action

- **Misreading Revelation:**

    o   Symbolic visions were treated as literal forecasts

What Was Hijacked

- **The Present Kingdom** *(Luke 17:21; Matthew 6:10)*:

    o   Replaced by future escape

- **The Incarnation** *(John 1:14)*:

    o   Replaced by rapture theology

- **The Mission of the Church** *(Matthew 25:35–40)*:

    o   Replaced by sky-watching and speculation

- **Hope as Healing** *(Romans 8:19–23)*:

    o   Replaced by hope as evacuation

The Distortion

- The Gospel became **an exit strategy**, not **a call to embody love**

- Suffering was seen as **prophetic fuel**, not **a summons to compassion**

- Jesus was portrayed as **coming to rescue the few**, not **restore the whole**

- The Church became **passive**, not prophetic

"Jesus didn't teach escape—He taught incarnation. He didn't say 'watch the sky,' He said 'feed the hungry.' The end isn't about fleeing the world—it's about redeeming it."

Echo #10: Christian Nationalism

"Empire baptized where kingdom once beckoned." This is empire theology masquerading as divine destiny.

Where It Happened

- **From Constantine to the present**, but intensified in **modern America**

- Key milestones:

  - **Constantine (4th century):** fused Church with imperial power

  - **Puritan colonists:** saw America as a "New Israel"

  - **Manifest Destiny (19th century):** framed expansion as divine mission

  - **Modern Evangelicalism:** fused patriotism with theology

o **Project 2025 & political movements**: seek to embed Christian dominance in law and governance

Who Was Involved

- **John L. O'Sullivan**: coined *Manifest Destiny*, linking nationalism to divine favor

- **Doug Wilson & Reformed leaders**: advocate "Mere Christendom" as political theology

- **Political figures & movements**: use Christian identity to justify exclusion, control, and dominion

- **Critics**: theologians, historians, and activists exposing its anti-Christ nature

Driving Force Behind the Shift

- **Power Cloaked in Piety**:

  o Faith became a tool to justify conquest, control, and exclusion

- **Fear of Decline**:

  o As Christianity's cultural dominance waned, nationalism surged as a defense

- **Theological Confusion**:

  o The kingdom of God was conflated with national greatness

- **Supremacy & Patriarchy**:

    o Christian nationalism often overlaps with racial, gender, and cultural hierarchies

What Was Hijacked

- **The Kingdom of God** *(Luke 4:43; John 18:36)*:

    o Replaced by nationalistic dominion

- **The Global Body of Christ** *(Galatians 3:28; Revelation 7:9)*:

    o Replaced by ethnocentric identity

- **The Way of the Cross** *(Philippians 2:5–8)*:

    o Replaced by triumphalism and coercion

- **The Mission of Love and Justice** *(Micah 6:8; Matthew 5)*:

    o Replaced by political conquest

The Distortion

- Jesus was rebranded as **a nationalist**, not **a servant-king**

- The Church became **a voting bloc**, not **a prophetic witness**

- Faith was weaponized to **exclude**, not to **embrace**

- The Gospel was twisted into **a mandate for control**, not **a message of liberation**

"The kingdom of God is not red, white, and blue. It's righteousness, peace, and joy in the Holy Spirit. Christian nationalism is empire theology—it crucifies Christ again in the name of Caesar."

Echo #11: Gender Hierarchy

"Divine image fractured where mutual glory once shone." How patriarchy distorted the imago Dei and silenced half the voice of the Spirit.

Where It Happened

- **Post-Fall reinterpretation**, institutionalized from **2nd century onward**

- Key milestones:

    o **Genesis 3:16** misread as divine prescription rather than curse

    o **Church Fathers** like Tertullian and Augustine: framed women as morally and spiritually inferior

    o **Medieval theology**: excluded women from leadership and sacramental authority

    o **Modern complementarianism**: codified male headship as divine design

Who Was Involved

- **Early theologians**: interpreted Eve's creation and fall as justification for male dominance

- **Church councils**: barred women from priesthood and decision-making

- **Reformers and Evangelicals**: reinforced gender roles through selective exegesis

- **Modern critics**: egalitarian theologians, feminist scholars, and Spirit-led reformers challenging the distortion

Driving Force Behind the Shift

- **Fear of Female Agency**:

  o Women's voices were seen as threats to doctrinal control

- **Cultural Patriarchy**:

  o Male dominance in society was baptized as divine order

- **Misreading of Scripture**:

  o Descriptive texts were treated as prescriptive mandates

- **Institutional Preservation**:

  o Silencing women preserved hierarchical power structures

What Was Hijacked

- **Imago Dei in All Humanity** *(Genesis 1:27)*:

  o Replaced by male-centric reflection of God

- **Mutual Submission and Partnership** *(Ephesians 5:21; Galatians 3:28)*:

  o Replaced by unilateral authority

- **Prophetic Voice of Women** *(Judges 4; Acts 2:17–18)*:

    o   Replaced by silence and subordination

- **Embodied Wisdom** *(Proverbs 8; Luke 1)*:

    o   Replaced by suspicion and exclusion

The Distortion

- God was portrayed as **exclusively male**, distorting divine fullness

- Women were cast as **helpers**, not co-heirs

- The Spirit's voice in women was **muted**, not magnified

- The Church became **a male echo chamber**, not a symphony of shared glory

"The curse was never the blueprint. Jesus shattered hierarchy—not reinforced it. The Spirit fell on sons and daughters alike, and the image of God was never gendered."

Echo #12: Suppression of the Spirit

"Presence silenced where fire once fell." This is the echo that runs beneath them all, the one that empire, hierarchy, and dogma have tried hardest to bury.

Where It Happened

- **From Acts to now**, but intensified through **institutional religion**

- Key milestones:

    o **Post-Pentecost**: spontaneous Spirit-led gatherings gave way to structured liturgy

    o **4th century onward**: Church aligned with empire, quenching prophetic spontaneity

    o **Reformation**: replaced Spirit-led revelation with sola scriptura alone

    o **Modern denominations**: turned Spirit baptism into tribal identity or theological controversy

Who Was Involved

- **Church Fathers**: emphasized order over Spirit-led chaos

- **Institutional leaders**: feared the unpredictability of the Spirit

- **Pentecostal movements**: reclaimed the fire, but often re-domesticated it

- **Modern gatekeepers**: regulate gifts, prophecy, and spontaneity through doctrine and control

Driving Force Behind the Shift

- **Fear of Disorder**:

    o Spontaneity was seen as threat to orthodoxy

- **Desire for Control**:

    o Spirit's voice was too wild, too democratic, too unpredictable

- **Theological Reductionism:**
  - Spirit became a doctrine, not a living presence
- **Cultural Respectability:**
  - Charisma was sanitized to fit polite religion

What Was Hijacked

- **The Birth of the Church** *(Acts 2)*:
  - Replaced by denominational branding and doctrinal gatekeeping
- **Prophetic Voice** *(Joel 2:28; 1 Corinthians 14)*:
  - Replaced by scripted sermons and censored gifts
- **Spontaneous Worship** *(John 4:23–24)*:
  - Replaced by performance and programming
- **Living Communion** *(2 Corinthians 13:14)*:
  - Replaced by ritual and routine

The Distortion

- The Spirit became **a doctrine**, not **a daily companion**
- Prophecy became **a liability**, not **a lifeline**
- Worship became **a production**, not **a participation**
- The Church became **a building**, not **a burning bush**

"The Spirit was never meant to be managed. He is wind, fire, breath, and voice. He births the Church—not through policy, but through presence."

These twelve echoes form a constellation of distortion—but they also point to a deeper truth: the Royal Gospel is not lost. It's buried beneath centuries of rubble, waiting to be uncovered, lived, and proclaimed. A call to awaken, to remember, and to reclaim. It's the voice of the Royal Gospel rising from the rubble, shaking off centuries of distortion, and declaring the kingdom that never died.

A Declaration of Restoration

Redeeming the Royal Gospel from the Echoes of Hijack

We stand at the threshold of remembrance.
Not to mourn what was lost, but to resurrect what was buried.
The Royal Gospel—the living proclamation of Christ's Finished Work, the indwelling Spirit, and the present kingdom—was never defeated.
It was hijacked. Distorted.
Buried beneath empire, dogma, and fear.
But now, it rises.

We Declare the Twelve Echoes Exposed

1. **Constantine's Imperial Adoption of Christianity**
   We reject the fusion of throne and altar. The kingdom of God is not built by conquest—it is revealed by love.

2. **Replacement of *Ecclesia* with Institutional "Church"**
We reclaim the called-out assembly. The Church is not a building—it is a body, a family, a Spirit-led people.

3. **The Clergy-Laity Divide**
We dismantle hierarchy. Every believer is a priest, a temple, a bearer of glory mirroring our King. Leadership is service, not control.

4. **The Doctrine of Original Sin**
We restore original blessing. Humanity was made in divine image, not born in guilt. Christ revealed our belovedness, not our depravity.

5. **Penal Substitution**
We reject wrath-based atonement. The cross was not divine vengeance—it was divine vulnerability. Love poured out, not punishment absorbed.

6. **Eternal Conscious Torment**
We silence the lie of endless agony. Judgment is restorative, not retributive. God's justice heals—it does not torture.

7. **Sacramental Gatekeeping**
We open the table. Grace is not rationed—it flows freely. Baptism, communion, and fellowship belong to all who breathe the Spirit.

8. **Biblical Literalism**
We honor the living Word. Scripture is not a cage—it is a canvas. The Spirit still speaks, still breathes, still reveals.

9. **End Times Obsession**

   We reject escapism. The kingdom is here, now. We do not flee the world—we redeem it. Hope is not evacuation—it is incarnation.

10. **Christian Nationalism**

    We sever the gospel from empire. Jesus is not a mascot for political power—He is the servant-king of a borderless kingdom.

11. **Gender Hierarchy**

    We restore mutual glory. Male and female reflect the image of God together. The Spirit speaks through sons and daughters alike.

12. **Suppression of the Spirit**

    We unchain the wind. The Spirit is not a doctrine—He is breath, fire, voice, and presence. He births the Church, not institutions.

We Call Forth the Restoration

- A gospel of **union**, not transaction

- A kingdom of **presence**, not performance

- A Church of **family**, not hierarchy

- A theology of **love**, not fear

- A movement of **Spirit**, not control

We are not reforming religion.
We are resurrecting reality.

We are not polishing the old wineskin.
We are pouring new wine into the living body of Christ.

We Proclaim

The Royal Gospel is not a theory—it is a truth.
It is not a doctrine—it is a declaration.
It is not a future hope—it is a present reality.

Christ has finished the work.
The Spirit has been poured out.
The kingdom is within us.

Let the echoes fall silent.
Let the roar of restoration rise.

The Ever-Increasing Kingdom: From Distortion to Restoration

"Of the increase of His government and peace there shall be no end..." — Isaiah 9:7

I. The Distortion — When Religion Replaced the Kingdom

For centuries, the gospel has been misrepresented—not as a declaration of divine government, but as a system of religious control. What began as a radical announcement of liberation was slowly domesticated into institutional dogma. The message of Christ was never meant to produce passive believers waiting for heaven—it was meant to activate sons and daughters who embody heaven now.

- **Dogma taught delay**: "Someday Jesus will return and fix everything."

- **Systems taught separation**: "God is holy, you are not—earn your way back."

- **Leaders taught dependence**: "You need us to mediate your access to God."

But Jesus didn't come to reinforce separation—He came to end it. He didn't come to start a religion—He came to reveal a kingdom. And that kingdom is not postponed until the Second Coming. It is present, increasing, and unstoppable.

As Jesus said to the Pharisees, "You shut the door of the kingdom of heaven in people's faces" (Matt. 23:13). The distortion is not just theological—it's governmental. It has kept people out of the very reality Christ died to bring near.

II. The Restoration — Love as Heaven's Government

The kingdom of God is moving us toward a glorious eschatology. The end cannot be tragic if His government and peace never cease increasing. And that kingdom is governed by love—not law, not fear, not hierarchy. Love is the government of heaven. It dignifies, restores, and empowers. It doesn't demand allegiance—it awakens identity.

- **Jesus didn't come to take sides—He came to take over.**

- **The cross wasn't a rescue mission—it was a coronation.**

- **The resurrection wasn't a future promise—it was a present activation.**

Isaiah's prophecy doesn't speak of a stagnant reign—it speaks of increase. The government of Christ is not static—it's expanding. And what fuels that expansion is not control, fear, or hierarchy. It's love.

Love is not a sentiment—it's the infrastructure of heaven. It dignifies the broken, restores the fallen, and empowers the weak. It doesn't demand allegiance—it awakens identity. As Paul wrote, "Love is the fulfillment of the law" (Rom. 13:10). And Jesus declared, "By this everyone will know that you are My disciples—if you love one another" (John 13:35).

The cross was not merely a rescue mission—it was a regime change. The resurrection was not a future promise—it was a present activation. The Finished Work of Christ is not a theological footnote—it's the foundation of a new world.

This is the restoration: not a return to Eden, but a revelation of the kingdom. Not a rebuilding of religious systems, but a rebirth of divine government—where love rules, peace multiplies, and justice flows like a river.

The Finished Work of Christ is not just theological—it's governmental. It declares that everything needed for restoration has already been accomplished. We're not waiting for Jesus to return—we're revealing the reality He already established.

III. The Activation — You Are the Increase

Isaiah 9:7 doesn't say His government will appear someday. It says it will increase. That means it's already here—and growing. But how? Through you.

You are not a spectator in this story. You are a participant. A co-heir. A carrier of the kingdom. Scripture declares,

- **You are seated with Christ (Eph 2:6)**—not someday, but now.

- **You are complete in Him (Col 2:10)**—not lacking, not waiting.

- **You are the body of Christ (1 Cor 12:27)**—not metaphorically, but manifestly.

The increase of His government is not happening around you—it's happening through you. Every act of love, every declaration of truth, every dismantling of religious distortion is kingdom expansion.

Creation is not waiting for Jesus to descend—it's waiting for you to rise. "The whole creation waits in eager expectation for the revealing of the sons of God" (Rom. 8:19). The cloud of witnesses is not watching for the sky to split—they're watching for you to awaken. To activate. To embody the kingdom. Heaven is poised. Earth is groaning. And the Spirit is stirring a generation who will no longer wait for revival—they will *be* revival.

IV. The Convergence — One Spirit, Many Voices

This awakening is not isolated. It's converging. Across denominations, cultures, and continents, the Spirit is harmonizing a message: the Finished Work is not just a doctrine—it's a doorway. The veil is lifting. The ground is shifting. And the voices are rising.

Paul reminds us, "There are different kinds of gifts, but the same Spirit distributes them" (1 Cor. 12:4). Joel prophesied, "I will pour out My Spirit on all flesh" (Joel 2:28). This is that. The convergence is here.

- **Same Spirit, different faces.**

- Same truth, different tones.

- Same kingdom, increasing through love.

This is not a trend. It's a tectonic shift. The ground is moving. The veil is lifting. And the message is clear: *Christ is not coming to reign—He already reigns. Now we must reveal it.*

V. The Invitation — Step Into the Increase

This is the moment. Not to wait. Not to wish. But to walk. The invitation is not to observe the kingdom—it's to embody it. You are not waiting for revival—you are revival. You are not hoping for heaven—you are revealing it.

- **"Arise, shine, for your light has come, and the glory of the Lord rises upon you"** (Isa. 60:1).
- **"We are ambassadors of Christ"** (2 Cor. 5:20).
- **"By one offering He has perfected forever those who are being sanctified"** (Heb. 10:14).

So, speak truth that dismantles shame. Live love that reforms systems. Rest in the Finished Work. Rise in authority. Reveal the kingdom. This is not the end—it's the increase. And it begins with you. This is the moment. Not to wait. Not to wish. But to walk. The government of Christ is love. The peace of Christ is rest. And the increase is *you.*

Belief, Inclusion, and a Path Forward: The Unveiling of What's Already True

For centuries, the gospel has been preached as a conditional transaction: "If you believe, then you will be saved." This framing has subtly—but profoundly—shifted the emphasis from Christ's finished work to human response. It has turned belief into a prerequisite for truth, rather than a revelation of it.

But the gospel is not a proposal. It is a proclamation.

Jesus did not come to make salvation *possible*—He came to make it *actual*. His incarnation, death, resurrection, and ascension were not theoretical gestures. They were cosmic realities that reconciled the world to God. As Scripture declares, "God was in Christ reconciling the world to Himself, not counting their trespasses against them" (2 Corinthians 5:19). That reconciliation is not pending. It is finished.

The Distortion of "Belief"

The word "believe" has been misunderstood and misused. In many circles, it has been reduced to intellectual assent or religious compliance. But in its original context, *pisteuō* (Greek for "believe") means to entrust, to awaken, to rest in what is already true. Belief is not the cause of salvation—it is the awakening to it.

Unbelief does not make the gospel false. It makes it *unrealized*. The truth remains. The light shines. But the eyes must open.

To say "only believers are saved" is to misunderstand both salvation and belief. Salvation is not a reward—it is a restoration. And belief is not a gate—it is a window.

This distortion has led many to live in fear, striving to earn what has already been given. It has created a gospel of conditions rather than a gospel of completion. But the truth is this: belief does not activate salvation—it *reveals* it.

The Accusation of Universalism

Those who proclaim the full scope of Christ's finished work are often accused of universalism. The term itself is slippery—sometimes used to mean "everyone is automatically saved," other times to imply "truth doesn't matter." But these accusations miss the point entirely.

The true gospel is not indifferent to truth—it is *anchored* in it. It does not erase the need for awakening—it *invites* it. And it does not flatten human experience—it *redeems* it. To affirm that Christ reconciled the world is not to deny the importance of belief—it is to rightly place belief in its proper role. Belief is not the mechanism of salvation—it is the mirror that reveals it. We are not saying "everyone is saved regardless of Christ." we are saying "everyone is included *because* of Christ." This is not universalism—it is *universal inclusion*. The difference is profound.

- Universalism says: "It doesn't matter what you believe."

- Universal inclusion says: "It matters infinitely what Christ has done—and belief awakens you to it."

This message does not minimize the gospel—it magnifies it. It does not dilute the power of Christ—it declares it without limitation.

A Gospel of Honor

We must honor those who have risked their reputations to speak truth. Reformers across generations have peeled away centuries of fear-based theology to reveal the liberating love of the Father. Their message is not heresy—it is healing.

And we must also honor those still bound by old paradigms. Not with condescension, but with compassion. Many are sincere. Many are afraid. Many have never heard the gospel without the threat of hell attached. We do not shame them—we invite them.

This is not about winning arguments—it's about winning hearts. It's about restoring the dignity of the gospel and the people it was meant to liberate.

The Eternal Now

The gospel is not waiting for mass agreement to become true. It is true now. Christ is risen now. The Spirit indwells now. The Father loves now. And belief is the awakening to this eternal now. When all believe, it will be universal. But even now, it is already finished. This is the message:

- That salvation is not a transaction—it is a transformation.

- That belief is not a requirement—it is a revelation.

- That the gospel is not fear—it is freedom.

- That the work is not pending—it is finished.

And the increase of His government and peace will never end.

Awakening, Not Arguing—The Gospel's Impact on Evangelism, Discipleship, and Spiritual Formation

When the gospel is understood as the unveiling of what is already true—rather than a conditional offer—it transforms everything about how we engage the world. Evangelism becomes invitation, not persuasion. Discipleship becomes discovery, not indoctrination. Spiritual formation becomes alignment, not achievement.

Evangelism: From Pressure to Presence

Traditional evangelism often begins with a deficit: "You are lost, and here's how to get found." But when we start from the Finished Work, we begin with fullness: "You are loved, reconciled, and included—let me help you see it." This shift removes manipulation and restores dignity.

- We're not selling salvation—we're revealing it.

- We're not convincing people to accept Christ—we're awakening them to the Christ who already accepted them.

- We're not threatening hell—we're announcing heaven.

Evangelism becomes less about argument and more about *presence*. It's not a script—it's a spark. We carry the light, and when people encounter it, their eyes begin to open. This kind of evangelism is fearless and gentle. It doesn't rush. It doesn't coerce. It trusts the Spirit to do what only the Spirit can do: awaken hearts to truth.

Discipleship: From Control to Curiosity

Discipleship has often been framed as behavior modification or doctrinal conformity. But when we disciple from the Finished Work, we disciple from rest. We're not trying to get people to become something—they already are. We're helping them *see* it, *live* it, and *walk* in it. This kind of discipleship is:

- Rooted in identity, not performance.

- Fueled by love, not fear.

- Guided by curiosity, not control.

We don't hand people a checklist—we walk with them in discovery. We don't demand agreement—we cultivate awareness. We don't enforce hierarchy—we model humility. Discipleship becomes a journey of unveiling, where each person learns to trust the Spirit within them and live from their true self in Christ.

Spiritual Formation: From Striving to Surrender

Spiritual formation is not about becoming holy—it's about realizing you already are. It's not about climbing toward God—it's about sinking into union. When we form people spiritually from the Finished Work, we teach them to:

- Rest in grace, not strive for approval.

- Listen to the Spirit, not chase external validation.

- Embrace mystery, not fear it.

Spiritual maturity is not measured by how much you know—it's revealed in how deeply you love. It's not about mastering theology—

it's about embodying Christ. This kind of formation produces people who are:

- Free from shame.

- Anchored in love.

- Bold in truth.

- Gentle in spirit.

They don't need to be managed—they need to be trusted. Because the Spirit is already at work within them, forming Christ in them from the inside out.

The Ripple Effect

When evangelism, discipleship, and formation are rooted in the Finished Work, the ripple effect is profound:

- Communities become safe places of awakening, not battlegrounds of belief.

- Leaders become facilitators of freedom, not gatekeepers of doctrine.

- The Church becomes a living witness of reconciliation, not a fortress of exclusion.

This is not just a better method—it's a better message. It's the gospel as it was meant to be: liberating, loving, and already true.

From Hierarchy to Honor—Reimagining Leadership, Ecclesiology, and Societal Engagement

When the gospel is rightly understood as the proclamation of Christ's Finished Work and the universal inclusion of humanity, it doesn't just change personal faith—it reconfigures the entire landscape of leadership, church structure, and social responsibility. The implications are radical, restorative, and deeply human.

Leadership: From Control to Co-Creation

In many religious systems, leadership has been built on hierarchy—anointed few over the uninformed many. But when we lead from the Finished Work, we lead from *equality*, not elevation. Christ did not come to establish a chain of command—He came to restore a family.

- Leadership is not about power—it's about presence.

- It's not about being over—it's about being *with*.

- It's not about titles—it's about trust.

This kind of leadership honors the Spirit in every person. It listens more than it lectures. It equips rather than enforces. It creates space for others to rise, not platforms for self-preservation. Leaders become gardeners, not gatekeepers. They cultivate growth, protect dignity, and model vulnerability. They don't demand loyalty—they inspire love.

Ecclesiology: From Institution to Incarnation

The Church was never meant to be a fortress—it was meant to be a family. Not a system of control, but a community of Christ-consciousness. When ecclesiology is shaped by the Finished Work, it becomes:

- Fluid, not rigid.

- Relational, not institutional.

- Empowering, not excluding.

The Church is not the building—it's the body. And every member matters. Every voice is valued. Every gift is needed. We stop asking, "Who's in charge?" and start asking, "Who's being loved?"

This kind of ecclesiology dismantles the clergy/laity divide. It removes the pulpit pedestal. It decentralizes authority and recenters Christ. It becomes a living organism, not a dying organization. And most importantly, it becomes a safe place for awakening. A sanctuary for the soul. A launchpad for love.

Societal Engagement: From Separation to Solidarity

When we see humanity as already reconciled, we stop dividing the world into "us" and "them." We stop retreating from culture and start redeeming it. We stop preaching escape and start practicing incarnation. Societal engagement becomes:

- Justice rooted in mercy.

- Activism fueled by love.

- Advocacy shaped by dignity.

We no longer see the poor, the marginalized, the broken as "mission fields"—we see them as *family*. We don't serve to convert—we serve because we're connected.

This gospel doesn't just change hearts—it changes systems. It confronts oppression. It dismantles hierarchy. It restores equity. We become agents of reconciliation, not just in theology but in economics, education, healthcare, and governance. We carry the kingdom into every sphere—not to dominate, but to *liberate*.

The Reforming Pulse

This message reforms everything:

- Leadership becomes a dance of mutual honor.

- Church becomes a table, not a throne.

- Society becomes a canvas for kingdom expression.

And all of it flows from one truth: *It is finished.*

We don't lead to earn.
We don't gather to prove.
We don't engage to win.
We do all of it because love compels us.

This is the gospel unleashed.
This is the kingdom embodied.
This is the reformation we've been waiting for.

From Fragmented to Whole—The Gospel's Healing of Identity, Mental Health, and Emotional Wounds

When the gospel is stripped of fear, hierarchy, and conditions, it becomes what it was always meant to be: a balm for the broken, a mirror for the confused, and a home for the wandering. The Finished Work of Christ doesn't just reconcile us to God—it reconciles us to ourselves.

Identity: From Striving to Belonging

In a world obsessed with performance, titles, and external validation, identity has become a fragile construct. Many live with a fractured sense of self—trying to earn worth, prove value, or escape shame. But the gospel declares: *You are already known. Already loved. Already included.*

- You are not what you do.

- You are not what you've survived.

- You are not what others say.

You are who God says you are: beloved, whole, and one with Christ. This truth dismantles the false self. It silences the inner critic. It heals the orphan spirit. You don't have to hustle for identity—you inherit it.

When people awaken to this, they stop chasing roles and start embracing relationship. They stop asking, "Who should I be?" and start resting in, "I already am."

Mental Health: From Chaos to Clarity

The gospel has often been weaponized against mental health—treating anxiety as sin, depression as weakness, and trauma as spiritual failure. But this is not the heart of Christ.

The Finished Work says: *You are not broken—you are beloved.*

Mental health is not a threat to faith—it's a doorway to deeper healing. The gospel doesn't bypass the mind—it renews it. It doesn't shame emotion—it honors it. When we preach inclusion, we remove the fear of rejection. When we proclaim reconciliation, we silence the voice of condemnation. When we embody love, we create safe spaces for healing.

This message affirms:

- You are allowed to feel.

- You are allowed to struggle.

- You are allowed to heal slowly.

And through it all, you are never outside the embrace of God.

Emotional Healing: From Shame to Shalom

Shame is the great thief of peace. It convinces us we're unworthy, unlovable, and beyond repair. But the gospel of the Finished Work exposes shame for the lie it is.

Christ didn't just die for sin—He died to remove shame. He didn't just rise to conquer death—He rose to restore dignity. Emotional healing begins when we stop hiding and start receiving. When we stop performing and start resting. When we stop punishing ourselves and start believing the truth:

- You are not too much.

- You are not too far gone.

- You are not alone.

The Spirit is not afraid of your pain. He is present in it. And He is whispering, "You are mine."

This kind of healing is not a formula—it's a flow. It's not a quick fix—it's a lifelong embrace. And it's available to all, because *all are included*.

The Gospel as Therapy

This message becomes therapy for the soul:

- It restores identity.

- It affirms mental health.

- It heals emotional wounds.

It doesn't demand perfection—it invites presence. It doesn't rush the process—it honors it. It doesn't shame the struggle—it walks with it.

This is not just theology—it's transformation.
Not just doctrine—it's deliverance.
Not just belief—it's becoming.

And it all flows from one eternal truth: *It is finished.*

From Sacred to Seamless—The Gospel's Impact on Family, Creativity, Education, Economics, and More

When the gospel is rightly understood—not as a religious escape plan but as the unveiling of Christ's Finished Work—it doesn't stay confined to pulpits and prayer closets. It spills into kitchens, classrooms, studios, boardrooms, and city streets. It reorders everything, not by domination, but by *liberation*.

This is the gospel as integration—not separation. It's not just for Sunday—it's for *every moment*.

Family: From Obligation to Overflow

Family has often been shaped by duty, hierarchy, and inherited dysfunction. But when the gospel enters the home, it transforms family into a sanctuary of grace.

- Parents stop controlling and start cultivating.

- Children stop performing and start belonging.

- Marriages shift from survival to sacred union.

The Finished Work means every member of the family is already loved, already valued, already included. There's no need to earn affection or fear rejection. Love becomes the atmosphere, not just the aspiration.

This kind of family:

- Honors emotion.

- Practices forgiveness.

- Celebrates uniqueness.

- Models' mutual submission.

It becomes a living picture of the kingdom—a place where everyone is safe, seen, and free.

Creativity: From Fear to Flow

Creativity has often been stifled by religious rigidity or cultural pressure. But the gospel unleashes creativity as a divine impulse—a reflection of the Creator within.

When people awaken to their inclusion in Christ, they stop censoring their imagination and start trusting it. Art becomes worship. Innovation becomes intercession. Expression becomes embodiment.

This message affirms:

- You were made to create.

- Your voice matters.

- Your ideas carry divine spark.

Creativity is no longer a luxury—it's a necessity. It's how heaven touches earth. Whether through painting, poetry, music, design, or entrepreneurship, the gospel fuels fearless creation.

Education: From Indoctrination to Illumination

Education has often been used to control minds rather than awaken them. But when shaped by the Finished Work, education becomes a journey of discovery, not conformity. We stop asking, "What should they know?" and start asking, "Who are they becoming?"

This kind of education:

- Honors curiosity.

- Encourages questions.

- Affirms identity.

- Cultivates wisdom.

Teachers become guides, not gatekeepers. Students become explorers, not empty vessels. Learning becomes sacred, because every truth discovered is a glimpse of the One who holds all things together.

Economics: From Scarcity to Sufficiency

Economics has been driven by fear, competition, and exploitation. But the gospel reimagines economics as a system of shared abundance. The Finished Work declares: *There is enough.*

- Enough love.

- Enough dignity.

- Enough provision.

We stop hoarding and start sharing. We stop exploiting and start empowering. We stop measuring worth by wealth and start measuring it by love. This kind of economics:

- Prioritizes people over profit.

- Honors labor with justice.

- Redistributes power with equity.

- Builds systems that reflect the kingdom.

It's not socialism or capitalism—it's *kingdom economy*. Where generosity flows, and no one is left behind.

And More: The Gospel as Infrastructure

This message doesn't just touch isolated areas—it becomes the infrastructure of life.

- In politics, it calls for servant leadership and restorative justice.

- In healthcare, it affirms holistic healing and dignity for all.

- In technology, it inspires ethical innovation and connection.

- In media, it reclaims storytelling as a tool for truth and transformation.

The gospel is not a compartment—it's a current. It flows through everything. It doesn't demand withdrawal from the world—it empowers engagement with it.

The Seamless Gospel

This is the seamless gospel:

- It heals families.

- It fuels creativity.

- It reforms education.

- It reimagines economics.

- It reshapes society.

And it does all of this not by force, but by *freedom*. Not by fear, but by *love*. Not by striving, but by *resting* in the truth:

It is finished.

From Temporary to Timeless—The Gospel's Redemption of Time, Death, Legacy, and Eternity

The gospel is not just a message for the living—it's a revelation that transcends time itself. It speaks to the past, redeems the present, and unveils the eternal. When we awaken to the Finished Work of Christ, we stop fearing the clock and start living from eternity.

This is not escapism—it's embodiment. Not delay—it's divine immediacy.

Time: From Scarcity to Sacred Rhythm

Time has long been treated as a tyrant—something we race against, fear losing, or try to control. But the gospel reframes time as a gift, not a threat.

In Christ, time is not running out—it's being redeemed.

- The past is healed.

- The present is holy.

- The future is secure.

We stop living in regret or anxiety and start living in *kairos*—God's divine timing. Every moment becomes meaningful. Every breath becomes worship. Every season becomes sacred.

This message teaches us to:

- Slow down without guilt.

- Show up without fear.

- Trust the unfolding without panic.

Time is no longer a countdown—it's a canvas.

Death: From Finality to Fulfillment

Death has been the great fear, the looming unknown, the ultimate interruption. But the gospel declares: *Death has been defeated*.

Christ didn't just die—He dismantled death. He didn't just rise—He redefined reality.

When we live from the Finished Work:

- Death is not the end—it's a doorway.

- We don't fear it—we transcend it.

- We don't avoid it—we reframe it.

This truth doesn't minimize grief—it sanctifies it. It doesn't erase loss—it redeems it. We mourn with hope, not despair. We honor the departed, knowing they are not gone—they are *glorified*.

And we live with boldness, knowing that death cannot undo what Christ has already finished.

Legacy: From Achievement to Alignment

Legacy has often been measured by accomplishments, accolades, or influence. But the gospel redefines legacy as *alignment* with love.

Your legacy is not what you build—it's what you *embody*.

- It's the love you leave behind.

- The dignity you restore.

- The truth you carry.

- The freedom you spark.

You don't need a platform to leave a legacy—you need presence. You don't need fame—you need faithfulness. You don't need applause—you need authenticity.

This message empowers people to live lives that echo eternity—not by striving, but by *surrendering* to love.

Eternity: From Distance to Dwelling

Eternity has often been framed as a future reward—a distant paradise for the faithful few. But the gospel reveals eternity as a *present reality*.

Christ didn't come to offer heaven later—He came to unveil heaven *now*.

- Eternity is not a destination—it's a dimension.

- Not a someday—it's a *this day*.

- Not a reward—it's a *revelation*.

We are not waiting to enter eternity—we are already in it. The Spirit dwells within. The kingdom is at hand. The veil is torn.

This truth transforms how we live:

- We stop postponing joy.

- We stop fearing judgment.

- We stop delaying purpose.

We live from eternity, not toward it. We embody heaven on earth. We carry the divine into the mundane. We become portals of glory in everyday life.

The Eternal Echo

This message reverberates across time:

- It heals the past.

- It sanctifies the present.

- It secures the future.

- It unveils eternity.

And it does all of this because *it is finished*.

You are not running out of time.
You are not defined by death.
You are not forgotten in legacy.
You are not waiting for eternity.

You are *already included*.
Already loved.
Already alive in Christ.

This is the gospel that doesn't just save—it *sings*.
It doesn't just rescue—it *reigns*.
It doesn't just promise—it *permeates*.

And it's yours. Now. Forever.

From Institution to Incarnation—The Future of the Church in Light of the Finished Work

The Church has long been seen as the steward of the gospel. But when the gospel is rediscovered—not as a conditional offer, but as a cosmic declaration of reconciliation—the Church itself must be reimagined. The future of the Church is not about survival—it's about surrender. Not about preservation—it's about *presence*.

This is not the end of the Church. It's the end of the *old* Church. And the beginning of something far more beautiful.

The Crumbling of the Old Wineskin

The institutional Church, built on hierarchy, fear, and performance, is showing its cracks. Attendance declines. Scandals erupt. Trust erodes. But this is not failure—it's *refinement*. The shaking is mercy. The collapse is invitation.

The old wineskin cannot hold the new wine of the Finished Work.

- Systems built on separation cannot sustain a gospel of union.

- Structures built on control cannot contain a Spirit of freedom.

- Doctrines built on fear cannot coexist with perfect love.

The Church must die to what it was in order to rise into what it *is*.

The Rise of the Embodied Church

The future Church will not be defined by buildings, budgets, or branding. It will be defined by *embodiment*. Christ in us. Love through us. Kingdom among us.

This Church will be:

- Decentralized but deeply connected.

- Diverse but divinely unified.

- Unbranded but unmistakably Christlike.

It will gather in homes, parks, cafés, and online spaces. It will look less like a service and more like a family. Less like a performance and more like a presence.

Leadership will be shared. Gifts will be honored. The Spirit will be trusted.

This Church will not ask, "What do we believe?" but "How do we love?"
Not "Who's in charge?" but "Who's being healed?"
Not "How do we grow?" but "How do we *go*?"

The Church as Catalyst

The future Church will not exist to preserve itself—it will exist to *ignite* the world.

- It will be a catalyst for justice.

- A sanctuary for healing.

- A launchpad for creativity.

- A hub for reconciliation.

It will partner with educators, artists, activists, and entrepreneurs. It will speak truth to power and grace to the broken. It will dismantle systems of oppression and build communities of honor.

It will not retreat from culture—it will *redeem* it.

The Church as Living Organism

The Church will no longer be a static institution—it will be a living organism. Breathing. Moving. Multiplying.

It will be:

- Adaptive, not rigid.

- Relational, not hierarchical.

- Spirit-led, not program-driven.

It will embrace mystery. Celebrate nuance. Honor process. It will be safe for questions, bold in truth, and anchored in love.

And it will be unmistakably marked by one reality: *Christ is already here.*

The Church of the Eternal Now

The future Church will not wait for revival—it will *be* revival.
It will not preach delay—it will embody *now*.
It will not fear the future—it will *form* it.

This Church will live from the Finished Work.
It will proclaim reconciliation.

It will practice inclusion.
It will carry the increase of His government and peace.

And it will do all of this not to earn favor, but to express it.
Not to gain power, but to give it away.
Not to build empires, but to birth *Eden*.

The Invitation

The Church is not dying—it's *resurrecting*.
Not into what it was, but into what it was always meant to be.

You are part of that resurrection.
You are the Church.
You are the increase.
You are the unveiling.

This is the future.
And it is *already here*.

The Call to Alignment— Living the Reality of the Kingdom

The message of this book is not a new revelation—it is a long-overdue recognition. The kingdom of Christ did not begin with our awareness of it. It began with His Finished Work. The Spirit has been nudging, shaking, and awakening us for generations. Now, we respond—not to initiate a movement, but to *join* one already in motion.

This is not a call to innovate.
It is a call to *align*.
To live what has already been made true.
To embody what has already been given.

Recapping the Seven Movements

Each section of this book has revealed a facet of the kingdom's reality and the distortions that have obscured it:

1. **The Finished Work of Christ**: The foundation—complete, irreversible, and universal. We begin not with striving, but with rest.

2. **The Gospel of Reconciliation**: Not a conditional offer, but a cosmic declaration. We are not earning union—we are awakening to it.

3. **The Dismantling of Religious Hierarchy**: The veil is torn. The clergy-laity divide is abolished. All are priests. All are beloved.

4. **The Centrality of Love**: Love is not a virtue—it is the very nature of God. It reforms, restores, and reorders everything.

5. **The Restoration of Human Dignity**: Every person bears divine image. No one is disposable. The kingdom honors all.

6. **The Present Reality of the Kingdom**: Heaven is not a destination—it is a dimension. Christ reigns *now*. We live from that reign.

7. **The Future of the Church**: Not institutional preservation, but incarnational presence. The Church is becoming what it was always meant to be.

These are not isolated insights. They are a single, Spirit-breathed movement toward *alignment*.

The Path Forward

We are not building a new Church. We are *becoming* the Church that Christ already established.

We are not waiting for the kingdom. We are *walking* in it.

This path forward is marked by:

- **Surrender**: Letting go of control, fear, and performance.

- **Embodiment**: Living the truth, not just preaching it.

- **Participation**: Joining the Spirit's work in every sphere of life.

- **Honor**: Seeing Christ in every person, and treating them accordingly.

- **Creativity**: Expressing the kingdom through art, justice, business, and community.

- **Boldness**: Speaking truth with grace, and grace with truth.

This is not a program. It is a posture. Not a strategy. A surrender. Not a revival. A recognition.

The Call

So we say yes.
Yes to the Finished Work.
Yes to the Spirit's impulse.
Yes to the kingdom that is already here.

We reject delay theology.
We renounce religious control.
We release the need to be right, and embrace the call to be *real*.

We align. We awaken. We act.

Not to earn.
Not to prove.
But to *express* the love that has already claimed us.

This is the Church.
This is the kingdom.
This is the moment.

And it is *not ours to create*.
It is ours to *inhabit*.

The Truth about You

Eph 1:4 – You were found in Christ before you were lost in Adam.

2 Cor 5:15-17 – You are a new creation.

Eph 1:5 – You are Gods child.

Eph 2:6 – You are seated with Christ in heavenly places.

Gal 2:20 – The real you is Christ in you.

Col 2:10 – You are complete in Christ.

Rom 8:1 – There is no condemnation in Christ.

Rom 4:25 – You have been justified.

Rom 5:17-19 – You have been declared righteous.

Heb 10:14 – You have been made perfect forever.

Luke 10:19 – You have permission and power to shut down anything not aligned with the Kingdom.

1 John 4:17 – All that Jesus is now – so are we – in this world.

Eph 2:10 – You are fully equipped to do good.

Col 3:23 – Everything you do – do it unto the Lord Himself.

Gal 5:1 – It is for freedom sake Christ set you free!

Matt 11:28-30 – You can rest in Christ.

Col: 1:27 – Christ in you is the hope of glory.

The Truth about You

Eph 1:4 – You were found in Christ before you were lost in Adam.

Religion starts the story with sin. But God starts it with union. You were chosen in Christ before failure ever entered the scene. The lie says you're trying to get back to God; the truth says you've never been outside His heart. The Finished Work reveals that redemption isn't a rescue mission—it's a revelation of what's always been true.

---

2 Cor 5:15–17 – You are a new creation.

Dogma says you're a sinner trying to behave. But the gospel says you're a new creation—reborn, redefined, and re-rooted in Christ. The old is not just forgiven; it's gone. The Finished Work doesn't improve the old you—it unveils the real you.

Eph 1:5 – You are God's child.

Religion makes you earn sonship through obedience. But the truth is: you were adopted in love, not performance. You're not a servant climbing toward approval—you're a child resting in belonging. The Finished Work secures your identity, not your résumé.

Eph 2:6 – You are seated with Christ in heavenly places.

The system says you must ascend through effort. But grace says you're already seated. You don't climb ladders to reach God—you sit in union with Him. The Finished Work ends the striving and begins the reigning.

Gal 2:20 – The real you is Christ in you.

Religion teaches self-denial as self-erasure. But the gospel reveals that your true self is divine partnership. You're not empty—you're inhabited. The Finished Work doesn't suppress you—it reveals Christ alive in you.

Col 2:10 – You are complete in Christ.

Dogma says you're lacking, needing more rituals, more rules, more repentance. But the truth says you are complete. Nothing missing. Nothing broken. The Finished Work fills every gap religion tries to exploit.

Rom 8:1 – There is no condemnation in Christ.

Religion thrives on guilt. But the gospel silences it. You are not under judgment—you are under grace. The Finished Work doesn't just forgive—it removes the courtroom entirely.

Rom 4:25 – You have been justified.

The lie says you must prove your worth. But justification means the verdict is already in. You're not on trial—you're declared righteous. The Finished Work ends the case before it begins.

Rom 5:17–19 – You have been declared righteous.

Religion says righteousness is earned. But the gospel says it's gifted. You reign in life not because you're good—but because He is. The Finished Work makes righteousness your starting point, not your goal.

Heb 10:14 – You have been made perfect forever.

Dogma fears this verse. Religion says "not yet." But the gospel says "already." You've been made perfect—not by effort, but by one sacrifice. The Finished Work doesn't wait for your improvement—it declares your completion.

Luke 10:19 – You have permission and power to shut down anything not aligned with the Kingdom.

Religion teaches passivity. But Jesus gave authority. You're not a victim of circumstance—you're a vessel of dominion. The Finished Work empowers you to silence every lie, every fear, every force that opposes love.

---

1 John 4:17 – All that Jesus is now—so are we—in this world.

The system says "be like Jesus someday." But the truth says you already are. You're not becoming—you're revealing. The Finished Work doesn't delay your identity—it delivers it.

Eph 2:10 – You are fully equipped to do good.

Religion says you're unworthy to serve. But grace says you're handcrafted for impact. You're not a broken tool—you're a masterpiece in motion. The Finished Work equips you to live love out loud.

Col 3:23 – Everything you do—do it unto the Lord Himself.

Dogma divides sacred and secular. But the gospel unites it. Every act becomes worship. Every moment becomes ministry. The Finished Work sanctifies your ordinary into divine partnership.

Gal 5:1 – It is for freedom's sake Christ set you free!

Religion fears freedom. It prefers control. But Christ died to unleash it. You're not bound by fear, law, or shame—you're free to live, love, and walk in Spirit. The Finished Work is your emancipation proclamation.

Matt 11:28–30 – You can rest in Christ.

Dogma demands hustle. But Jesus invites rest. You're not called to carry religion—you're called to collapse into grace. The Finished Work is your Sabbath, your sanctuary, your soul's exhale.

Col 1:27 – Christ in you is the hope of glory.

Religion says glory is far off. But the gospel says it's within. Christ in you isn't a metaphor—it's the miracle. The Finished Work puts heaven in your chest and hope in your hands.

www.FinishedWorkofChrist.com

www.ingramcontent.com/pod-product-compliance
Lightning Source LLC
Jackson TN
JSHW081516261225
96021JS00001BA/1